THE Lighter STEP-BY-STEP INSTANT POT® COOKBOOK

ALSO BY
JEFFREY EISNER
*The Step-by-Step
Instant Pot
Cookbook*

THE
Lighter
STEP-BY-STEP
INSTANT POT®
COOKBOOK

Jeffrey Eisner

PHOTOGRAPHY BY ALEKSEY ZOZULYA

VORACIOUS

LITTLE, BROWN AND COMPANY
NEW YORK / BOSTON / LONDON

Voracious / Little, Brown and Company
Hachette Book Group
1290 Avenue of the Americas, New York, NY 10104
littlebrown.com

First Edition: April 2021

Voracious is an imprint of Little, Brown and Company, a division of Hachette Book Group, Inc. The Voracious name and logo are trademarks of Hachette Book Group, Inc.

INSTANT POT® and associated logos are owned by Instant Brands Inc. and are used under license.

The publisher is not responsible for websites (or their content) that are not owned by the publisher.

The Hachette Speakers Bureau provides a wide range of authors for speaking events. To find out more, go to hachettespeakersbureau.com or call (866) 376-6591.

Photographs by Aleksey Zozulya

All food styling by Carol J. Lee, except for Roasted Garlic & Spinach Soup, Eggplant Risotto, and Lemon Orzo Chicken: food styling by Jeffrey Eisner and Aleksey Zozulya; and White or Brown Rice: food styling by Sarah Constantino.

Interior design by Laura Palese

ISBN 978-0-316-70637-7
LCCN 2020946221

Printing 1, 2021

LSC-C

Printed in the United States of America

If you prefer a lighter eating lifestyle,
this book's for you.

If you want zero flavor compromise and
scrumptious satisfaction, this book's for you.

And to those who've struggled with weight
all their lives and want to eat healthier
without feeling like they are, you're my
people and this book's for you.

Everything in moderation, including moderation.

—OSCAR WILDE

CONTENTS

♨ = AIR FRYER LID
DF = DAIRY-FREE
K = KETO
GF = GLUTEN-FREE
P = PALEO
V = VEGETARIAN
+ = COMPLIANT WITH MODIFICATIONS
VN = VEGAN

INTRODUCTION

Waist Not, Want Not: My Wild Ride with Weight Loss

"Jeffrey, with all these recipes you make, how do you
not weigh 300 pounds?!"

I get that question a lot. And the truth is, I did once. It was
the year 2000, I was a sophomore in college, and stepping on the scale
racked up numbers like I had just bowled a perfect game. I was
19 years old. And I was (and still am) a food addict.

———

Remember Grandma Lil from my first book? She's the one who inspired my love of cooking. But I also inherited her struggle with weight. She was a pleasantly plump woman who loved to eat as much as she loved to cook.

When I began college and experienced my first taste of the freedom of living solo, I also experienced the freedom to eat anything I wanted, whenever I wanted. For me that meant bacon, egg, and cheese bagels for breakfast, two cheeseburgers and fries for lunch, a milkshake and chips for a snack, 24 buffalo wings for dinner, and a pair of ice cream sandwiches for dessert. Not to mention I drank bottles of soda like water. So it wasn't shocking that, in my case, the "freshman 15" was more the "freshman 50." I simply chose to ignore how much my belly and waist were expanding. I avoided mirrors and scales. I was in full denial.

But one day, after going up yet another pants size, I couldn't handle it anymore. I took a deep breath and decided to face myself in the mirror days before New Year's Eve. After a seriously sobering stare-down with that disappointed and depressed-looking young fella peering back at me, I decided to make a change. I set the goal that by my twentieth birthday, in six months' time, I would lose 100 pounds and take charge of my health.

And I did.

But it didn't happen overnight. I took a step aerobics class (remember those?) that met twice a week, walked everywhere on campus, danced (terribly) in a production of *The Pirates of Penzance*, and cut out all soft drinks. Above all else, I began to eat *lighter* and eat *less*. Gone were the days of polishing off a whole pizza at midnight or eating two grilled cheese sandwiches ... for a snack.

Come summer of 2001, I weighed 190 pounds (10 less than originally planned) and was the thinnest I'd ever been—and, more importantly, I felt the best I had felt in a long time. I went from a size 50 waist to a 34. I was wearing size medium T-shirts. Jaws dropped; people didn't recognize me. I felt like a new person and, for the first time in my life, I felt attractive.

Being a young lad of 20 with a healthy metabolism, I kept the weight off for a solid 8 years or so. But I eventually got lazy, my metabolism slowed, and the weight crept back—something I had vowed would never happen once I had lost all of it. Yet here I was, about to hit 30 and nearly back at square one. Before I hit the dreaded 300-pound mark again, I decided to get myself back on track and shed another 60 pounds. How? By doing the same thing as before. And it worked.

Since then, I've had ups and downs—periods of stress that threw me off my game and threatened the balance I've been able to achieve, times when it seemed like my efforts might all be for nothing. In a way, those efforts—the ongoing challenge of maintaining health when it gets hard—are where these recipes come from.

Over the course of my years-long struggle with weight, I learned that while it takes eating wisely, being mindful of portion control, and adding in some fitness for me to achieve weight loss, there are two absolutely key ingredients to doing it: *motivation* and *determination*. Without that drive, you can forget it. It won't happen. Believe me, I know. You need to *want* it for it to happen.

But now that you know this about me, let me be very clear:

This is *not* a book promising instant weight loss or how to follow a trendy diet (I hate that word by the way, so from now on let's call it a "lifestyle"). Nor am I a nutritionist or dietitian.

If you're familiar with my first book, you know that it was about how to get the most delicious, comforting food out of your Instant Pot. Many of those recipes are my favorites, but they aren't the only things I eat—not by a long shot. That's where these recipes come in.

Many people have written to ask me for healthier recipes than my standard comfort classics. And I wanted to deliver on these requests while catering to a range of lifestyles such as keto, paleo, gluten-free, dairy-free, vegetarian, and/or vegan.

But I didn't want this book to be called *The Healthy Step-by-Step Instant Pot Cookbook* because what is "healthy" anyway? It's such an abstract term, meaning different things to different people. Does it mean using less sugar or salt? Cutting out carbs completely? Eating only vegan? Running marathons four times a year? It's just too general, and everyone defines the term differently. One could call a bodybuilder who eats pounds of bacon healthy and another would call someone with curves who eats brown fried rice the same. Both can follow specific lifestyles that can achieve great results.

Personally, I define "healthy" as making conscious choices about which ingredients go into your food and eating the right amount at the right time. I truly feel that "healthy" is defined by how *you* see it, while employing common sense. But one thing is universal: knowing what you can and cannot eat is at the forefront of a lighter lifestyle.

This *is* a book about eating LIGHTER.

But if that's not your thing, don't let that word turn you off. It doesn't mean you can't still have the foods you love; you might just have to see them in a different, well, "light."

If there's anything I'm known for, it's how flavorful my recipes are. And folks, you're most definitely going to get that in this book. There are so many negative connotations to eating lighter—that the food tastes bland or terrible or involves ingredients you have no interest in eating in the first place. And that's understandable. I've seen too many kale smoothies I'd sooner water my plants with than drink.

This book's mission is to provide you with recipes that take a lighter approach to cooking *without sacrificing flavor*. As always, I call for accessible and affordable ingredients that will create absolutely delicious, satisfying meals that everyone will enjoy, but this time they'll be easier on the waistline. Even those who refuse to touch anything labeled "light," "healthy," or "low-fat" will come around when they learn the dish they just devoured also happens to be even slightly better for them as well.

Essentially, I'm talking recipes with loads of flavor that do your body a favor (yes, I do love my rhymes).

Don't get me wrong: I fully respect lifestyles that work for other people. If you've gone keto or dairy-free and have lost a bunch of weight and feel great, that's something to be incredibly proud of, but personally (and because fortunately for me I have no food allergies), following one strict lifestyle was never my thing. So, while this book won't focus on one specific lifestyle, I will indeed call out which recipes are specific-lifestyle-friendly.

Speaking of which, what do "keto" and "paleo" mean? And what about them are the same and different?

A *great* question. And one that can easily be explained, but with lots of possible leniencies and interpretations based on how one chooses to follow them. In preparation for writing this book, I've researched a lot on both of these lifestyles, as well as consulted friends who are on them and, truth be told, while there's definitely a consensus on the main points of what is and isn't allowed in each one, there are also many nuances on other smaller points. So in a nutshell, I'm going to lay out these details in the diligent way I gathered them, to the best of my knowledge. Keto and paleo are basically the same low-carb lifestyles except keto allows most dairy and doesn't typically allow natural sugars, whereas paleo is the opposite in those regards. A deeper dive on these, if you will.

KETO AND PALEO

Keto, short for *ketogenic,* is a lifestyle that encourages naturally high-fat foods and allows you to eat pretty much anything *except* carbs and sugar-heavy foods.

So all wheat products (breads, pastas), white and brown sugars (including starchy vegetables such as potatoes and many fruits; see the chart on page 12), grains (rice, quinoa), and legumes/beans are out the window. However, non-starchy veggies, proteins, dairy products (except fluid cow's milk), salt, and sugar substitutes (such as monk fruit sweetener, erythritol, stevia, and Swerve) are allowed. The reason fluid cow's milk (whole or skim) isn't especially keto-friendly is because it has a higher carb content due to the sugars it produces. But I know some keto lovers who are content with using small amounts in cooking. That being said, heavy cream and cheese, although a form of cow's milk, are different because they're higher in fat and lower in carbs.

Once you truly follow a lifestyle of only the allowed foods for a period of time, your body enters a state of "ketosis," which burns fat more regularly. However, the catch is that you really need to commit to this lifestyle. Technically if you eat a slice of classic pizza or have a bowl of pasta, you'll go out of ketosis. Falling off the wagon and doing a carb and/or sugar binge will make your body say *"What are you doing to me?!"* and it will revolt. As a result, you're likely to quickly gain back the weight you lost, and all the deprivation you endured may make you want to bang your head against a wall.

Paleo, short for *paleolithic,* is a diet that focuses on what cave people would have eaten based on what was available to them before humans had access to processed foods of any kind. As with keto, that means basically less carbs, white or brown sugars, grains, and beans/legumes. And, also like keto, nearly all proteins, non-starchy veggies, and salt are yours for the taking.

But unlike keto, with the exception of ghee (more on that on page 16), there's absolutely no dairy allowed on paleo. And you *can* eat natural sugars found in most fruits, as well as natural sweeteners such as monk fruit, erythritol, stevia, raw honey, pure maple syrup, and agave. As for other sweeteners, you can have all that keto allows with the addition of coconut sugar. I know this is a lot to take in and remember, and the lines can seem to blur in places so, to be clear, in my recipes if I call for either pure maple syrup or monk fruit sweetener in the ingredients list, you would use the former for paleo and the latter for keto *and* paleo. So, sweetly speaking, the paleo lifestyle is more lenient on natural sugars that can be used.

As for alcohol, that decision is subjective. I know many people on both keto and paleo who drink dry wine, light beer, and distilled spirits on occasion and have no problem cooking with them. But that's also entirely up to you. If a recipe calls for alcohol and you don't wish to use it, simply replace it with more broth.

The same strict commitment applies to paleo as for keto: you must remain dedicated to eating within the guidelines of the lifestyle to keep your results from backsliding. Whether or not these diets are sustainable for your lifestyle is up to you.

And yet, contrary to the points above, depending on who you ask and how seriously one follows these lifestyles is what determines what ingredients are okay for them to eat. Not everyone on keto cares about entering ketosis—they merely enjoy following the lifestyle moderately versus strictly. As with the alcohol situation, there are some folks who are perfectly fine with having a small amount of cornstarch or flour in a recipe that is dispersed among multiple servings. Some would say "Not even an ounce of carbs" and others would argue with "Well, a teaspoon of cornstarch is much better for me than eating a whole bagel!" (The latter is totally me.) It all depends on the person, how they view it, and how it works for them. The chart on page 12 shows the similarities and differences between the lifestyles.

All that said, I respect the keto and paleo lifestyles, as they've done wonders for many. But they are certainly not the only way to lead a healthy lifestyle. I personally don't follow them. What can I say? I like my carbs too much (but in moderation, of course).

PRO TIP

You'll notice in some recipes that I may suggest serving a keto- or paleo-compliant dish over rice or quinoa. Or I may show a plated dish with a side that isn't keto- or paleo-compliant, even though the recipe itself is (excluding, of course, any suggested sides or optional ingredients). So it is important to note that suggested sides are indeed suggestions. And any side dishes you serve should match the lifestyle you're following. For example, instead of rice, use cauliflower rice (see page 22). You can find what is and isn't keto- or paleo-compliant on the chart on page 12.

WHAT ABOUT GLUTEN-FREE?

As for a *gluten-free* lifestyle, you're looking at eating anything that *doesn't* contain any variety of wheat, barley, and rye, which cuts out many carbs, naturally making it a lower-carb lifestyle. Since we now live in a very gluten-conscious world thanks to an awareness of those with celiac disease and other sensitivities, many prepared food products have gluten-free versions (such as sauces, pastas, beers, and more). You can always check the packaging to see if an item is gluten-free. Read carefully, because many products can unexpectedly include wheat or gluten in some form.

While there are limitations, there are also many foods that a gluten-free lifestyle welcomes: rice (white or brown), seeds (quinoa), starchy veggies (potatoes), cornstarch, arrowroot, tapioca, buckwheat, and oats, to name a few.

EVERY BODY IS DIFFERENT

Some people can eat anything they want and have the good fortune of not gaining an ounce (like my sister—grrrr). I've found that people with a healthy approach to food and eating typically balance out the more indulgent foods by eating lighter meals in combination with regular fitness. When it comes to my own weight, I'm fine with a happy medium, and don't necessarily

FOOD	KETO	PALEO
Proteins (eggs, poultry, meat, seafood)	Yes	Yes
Healthy fats (olive oil, coconut oil, avocado, etc.)	Yes	Yes
Nuts and seeds (including unsweetened nut milks)	Yes	Yes
Dairy (butter, cheese, milk, creams)	Yes, except fluid cow's milk; heavy cream and cheese are okay	No to all except ghee
Non-starchy vegetables	Yes	Yes
Starchy vegetables (potatoes, corn, carrots, beets, squash)	No to all except carrots and most squash, which can be consumed in limited quantities	No to all except carrots and beets; squash and sweet potatoes are okay in moderation
Most fruits	No, except for small servings of most berries, cantaloupe, peaches, and watermelon; lemon and lime are fine	Yes
Natural sugar substitutes (monk fruit, erythritol, raw stevia, coconut sugar)	Yes, except for coconut sugar	Yes
Natural sweeteners (raw honey, pure maple syrup, agave)	No	Yes
White or brown sugar	No	No
Grains (rice, wheat, wheat flours, rye, oats, etc.)	No	No
Legumes (beans, lentils, split peas)	No	No

have any desire to return to my lowest weight back when I was a spry 20-year-old. To that point, I never go by those old-school doctor's office waiting room charts that tell you what your weight should be based on your height. I find these antiquated and ignorant because every person isn't built the same. Just because you share the same height as someone else hardly means your bodies should be the same weight. The point is, once *you* feel good about how you look and feel, then you've hit your goal!

If losing weight is what you've set out to do, once you begin to develop a healthier approach to food, you'll find that a successful weight loss journey isn't all about deprivation. We are all built differently, with different metabolisms, so everyone's journey is going to be a little different, but portion control along with a steady element of fitness is a great foundation for success.

Living DEEPly

Allow me to elaborate on the specifics of a lighter lifestyle. For the sake of fun acronyms, let's call it the DEEP-end lifestyle, focusing on the following:

Determination
Eating Wisely
Exercise
Portion Control

DETERMINATION

The path to a healthier lifestyle isn't always going to be easy, and sometimes you can be your own worst enemy—but you can also be your own best cheerleader, and that's where determination comes in to see that you achieve your goal. Find out what keeps you on track and motivated, and stick to those things. For example,

I eat the healthiest when I plan out my meals for the week and when I refrain from buying the snacks and sweets that I know I have the hardest time saying no to when a craving hits. (*Pro tip:* try not to go to the grocery store when you're hungry.)

While the scale can be a motivator for some, also pay attention to other factors as you continue your health journey. Long-lasting changes won't happen overnight, but you may eventually begin to notice changes in other areas. Maybe your jeans feel just a little bit looser. Maybe you notice you have more energy throughout the day, or you make it a couple extra blocks on your next run. Maybe you'll even notice yourself craving healthier options and making smarter food decisions. Personally, my check-ins happen with the mirror, although I understand this can be tricky for some. But essentially, if I feel good inside and out, I know I'm on the right track. Feeling happy and healthy is much more rewarding and motivating than an arbitrary number on a scale.

Just bear in mind that when you do begin a journey of losing weight and cutting out problematic items your body is used to welcoming, it will begin to get a little sassy with you. Sort of like my dog, Banjo, begging for table scraps, and me refusing to give him any. This is when your determination is put to the test the most. DO NOT GIVE IN AND DO NOT GIVE UP. This is happening because your body is adjusting to the new fuel you're feeding it, like fewer bad sugars, carbs, or high-fat content, not to mention there's more room in your stomach that's used to being filled.

As you transition to newer, healthier habits, your body will eventually get used to the new ways you're serving it. Your stomach will most likely begin to shrink and get filled more easily. And once you begin to notice changes, you'll become that much more determined to stay on this path.

From buying yourself a brand-new workout outfit to getting excited about cooking with seasonal fruits and vegetables, we all have different ways of getting motivated. I encourage you to experiment and find yours!

EXERCISE

This is the one that some people dread (including myself sometimes). But an element of fitness in our lives is so important. It can be something as simple as taking a walk around the block, or more intensive, like working out at the gym, using an elliptical or treadmill, or going to an all-out fitness bootcamp with a trainer screaming at you. When you find the exercise plan that works best for you, not only does it burn off stress and help you release any pent-up frustration, it can also encourage you to make better decisions in every part of your life.

While everyone should exercise at their own pace, I've found that devoting 45 minutes three days a week is the best commitment for me.

But how can you make a workout more fun and less like a workout? My tip is that while on a cardio machine, in addition to listening to your favorite music (why yes, I *have* worked out to Barbra Streisand and Broadway soundtracks), try watching your favorite TV shows on your phone or videos on your favorite YouTube channel (cough cough). We have more access to technology than ever before—take advantage of it. The time will fly by.

EATING WISELY

Our decisions around food are linked to more than just how much we weigh: food choices factor into mood, sleep, motivation, ability to concentrate, life span, relationships, and more. So while I would never dream of suggesting you give up red meat or pasta (in fact, they're proudly represented in this book), perhaps these lighter yet super tasty recipes can help you reconsider the small choices you make every day. For example, instead of filling my belly right before bed, I try not to eat a large meal during the four hours before I go to sleep. I find that if I do, I wake up feeling sluggish and full (I call this "a brick in the stomach"), which isn't exactly how I want to begin my day— especially if I have a lot to accomplish. If I'm hungry and want a snack, some carrots, a sugar-free ice pop, or a handful of a snack like Pirate's Booty is perfect.

Eating wisely isn't about deprivation, it's about appreciating a balance between enjoying the things you love and taking care of yourself and your body. Well, balance and maybe a tiny bit of self-control...

Which leads me to the "P" of the DEEP lifestyle.

PORTION CONTROL

Media these days is filled with fad diets (I'll use that dreaded word here) and restrictive guidelines for losing weight. In reality, learning to eat in moderation is one of the most important steps you can take toward a healthier lifestyle. For example, say you love pizza, but you've read that in order to slim down or maintain your weight, you can never have pizza again, so now you're miserable and having dreams about dancing pizzas to fill the void. Instead, what if you could stick to just two slices of the pie, in moderation (meaning not every day of the week, but every so often), and balance that out with light, healthy meals on the other days? That way you still get to enjoy a food you love while you maintain your healthy goals and leave behind the whole food-guilt mindset. This is exactly what I do when I'm slimming down myself.

Same thing goes for the recipes in this book. Although they are lighter—you won't find herb cream

You can be healthy at any size—for me, following the DEEP model helped me shed 20 pounds, as shown on the right.

cheese and heavy dairy this time around—taking note of serving sizes and listening to your body's signs that it is full is key. No matter how much lighter a recipe is compared to a comfort food, eating mindfully is still important.

As one who can be prone to shovel food into his mouth and be on his second helping while others are just midway through their first, I speak from experience when I say that eating more slowly is a crucial part of getting used to eating smaller portions. Making the food last longer and giving your body a chance to digest will also help make sure it resonates that it's being fed and content. Take a minute, breathe in between bites, talk to the person you're eating with, and then go for the next bite. Try not to get too ahead of them while they're eating. After all, you want your meal to last as long as theirs since you're sitting at the same table, right? Otherwise, you'll just be sitting there, eyeing their portion and picking off their plate as they stare you down (guilty as charged). If you're eating alone, take a minute to answer those unanswered emails in between bites.

A Word on Nutrition Info

In addition to asking me to write a lighter cookbook, a lot of folks also requested nutrition info in my recipes, and since this is indeed a book focused on lighter eating, I made sure that nutrition counts were included here. I want to explain this section very clearly so you can understand how I wrote the "rules" of this book.

Each recipe states the number of suggested servings, and the nutrition info reflects the amounts for each serving, not including any optional ingredients, toppings, or accompaniments. To elaborate, when I calculated the nutrition info, if there's an "or" in the ingredient list, it is the first ingredient listed that counts in the info. And if an ingredient states that it's optional, it's the typical cookbook norm to *not* include that in the nutrition info either since it's, well, "optional." That also means that the lifestyle icons won't take that ingredient into account. So if you see that Parmesan cheese is an optional ingredient in a recipe, as in my Roasted Garlic & Spinach Soup (page 84), the dish will still be considered dairy-free and won't include the cheese in the nutrition info.

Speaking of which, all of the nutrition info for each recipe was gathered by using a reputable, online nutrition calculator. As such, this means that it is all *generally* calculated and that it can vary slightly (or greatly) based on a brand you use. Therefore, *always be sure to read the label on any product you buy!* If you need to make sure it doesn't contain gluten, read the label (most products these days are quick to call that out right on the front for you). Same with any other ingredient you may not want, like certain sugars. For instance, some brands of mustards have added sugars or chemical sugars, and some don't. And when my recipes call for broths or canned tomato products, I always use low-sodium and no-salt-added, respectively. Both are very easy to find in many markets. However, if you get the regular version, it's perfectly fine—just know you'll have a little more sodium in your recipe. But not to worry! Even though I use lower-sodium ingredients in this book, the herbs and spices I use make up for it in rich flavor!

Also, you'll notice that some of the ingredients in my recipes call for an "either/or" situation. For instance, you may see pure maple syrup (to make it paleo) *or* monk fruit sweetener (to make it keto, while still being paleo); ghee (if dairy isn't an issue) *or* olive oil (to make it dairy-free). So I also sometimes give a little note next to a lifestyle icon with a "+" to call out which ingredient to use to make it lifestyle-compliant. Furthermore, the "+" will also consider the recipe to be compliant to a particular lifestyle as written with a little leniency if, say, using a cornstarch slurry in a keto or paleo recipe. Of course, use these ingredients only if they are acceptable to you. It's important for me to be transparent and let you know it may deviate from that lifestyle should one be hardcore about it (in other words: just don't use the slurry). There are only a few

recipes in this book that don't have any of the lifestyle icons. But that has zero reflection on the recipe being lighter! Just because something isn't keto or gluten-free does not make it bad for you.

Finally, whenever nondairy milk is called for in a recipe, I always use unsweetened almond milk as the default for the nutrition info.

Now, allow me to introduce you to your new pantry pals!

Your New Best Friends (or, Substitutions for Lighter Cooking)

Since this book shines a spotlight on lighter cooking, I was faced with the challenge of substituting healthier key ingredients and flavor bombs for those that are more indulgent, without compromising the flavor and overall appeal of the dish. Luckily, there are glorious solutions readily accessible. Here's a breakdown of the most important ingredients you should have in your pantry for making these wonderful recipes.

DAIRY

In my first cookbook, I generally used salted butter and heavy cream in my recipes. While these are welcomed in the keto community, not everyone is into that. So I've replaced the heavier with the lighter, meaning ghee, Greek yogurt (typically 2%), half-and-half, or dairy-free substitutes. Let me dive into this a bit more in a fancy chart.

TYPICAL INGREDIENT	THE LIGHTER VERSION
Butter	Ghee (see page 39 for recipe)
Heavy cream and milk	Unsweetened nondairy milk (such as almond, cashew, oat, light coconut, or soy milk)
	Half-and-half
	Light cream
Sour cream	Greek yogurt (see page 36 for recipe)
	Low-fat or fat-free sour cream
Cream cheese or spreadable herb cheese (like Boursin and Alouette)	Greek yogurt (see page 36 for recipe)
Shredded cheese	Shredded low-fat cheese
	Shredded vegan cheese
Grated Parmesan cheese	Nutritional yeast

Ghee

Ghee is a salt-free clarified butter with no milk solids. Its origins are in ancient India; the word *ghee* is Sanskrit. It tastes almost exactly like regular butter (although it has a slightly nuttier flavor that lends a wonderful depth to dishes) and is a go-to sub for many people who follow a lighter lifestyle. It's also the only acceptable dairy product for those on a paleo diet since the milk solids are strained away. If you haven't used this before, it's going to become one of your new best friends.

You can easily make your own ghee using the recipe on page 39, or buy it at the market either in a solid state next to the butter or already melted in the oil aisle. I prefer to keep it solid and chilled in a mason jar.

Nondairy Milks

Unsweetened almond, cashew, coconut (use light), oat, and soy milks are all vegan, dairy-free, and lighter than dairy milk. They can also be cooked under pressure in an Instant Pot without curdling, although most of the time I usually add them just before serving for a finishing touch. If you're following a keto or paleo diet, make sure to read the label and choose nondairy milks that are compliant (oat milk isn't) and unsweetened, as some have sugars added. Also make sure the carton states it's not vanilla flavored or you'll have some interesting (and likely unwanted) flavors added to your dish! I find that oat milk is the thickest and closest sub to a heavy cream.

If these won't do the trick, you can absolutely go the slightly richer route and use 2% milk, skim milk, half-and-half, or light cream for a more indulgent take. (*Fun fact:* if you're following keto, it is actually encouraged to use heavy cream as it's high in fat and low in carbs.) Milk is never the star of a dish, just a key player in bringing it together. So if the thought of a lighter milk turns you off, just know that it won't be easy to taste it as distinctly as if you were drinking it straight.

Greek Yogurt

Greek yogurt is slightly tart on its own, but once you mix it into a sauce or add some flavorful spices to it for a dip, it becomes an ideal substitute for sour cream or, in some circumstances, heavy cream. I use 2% in most of my recipes that call for it, but if you want a richer body, you can go for whole. (*Another fun*

fact: for keto, plain, full-fat Greek yogurt is preferred over lower fat.) And if you want it as light as it gets and keto and paleo don't matter to you, you can use fat-free.

OIL

Since we often sauté as a first step before pressure cooking to unleash a wonderful foundation of flavor, you'll find oil in many of my recipes. Here, we focus on minimally processed oils that are better for you than the typical vegetable and canola oils.

TYPICAL INGREDIENT	LIGHTER VERSION
Canola or vegetable oil	Extra-virgin olive oil
	Avocado oil
	Coconut oil (refined)

Extra-Virgin Olive Oil

Extra-virgin olive oil is used in pretty much all my recipes that call for oil, mainly because it's one of the most nutritious oils around. It contains antioxidants and healthy fats and is rich in flavor. (Regular olive oil has the healthy benefits stripped out as it's refined, so stick with extra-virgin—hence the name, meaning "untouched" due to a natural extraction process.)

Avocado Oil

This is another oil made from one of the healthiest (and tastiest) fats around: the avocado. It's light in flavor with a slightly grassy tone and tastes more like olive oil once cooked. Avocado oil can be used interchangeably with extra-virgin olive oil in my recipes.

Coconut Oil

Coconut oil is another very popular and healthier oil. It's typically sold in a solid state and found next to the other oils or in the organic aisle of most markets. I strongly suggest getting the type that is labeled "refined" because it doesn't have a strong flavor of coconut. Not that the flavor of coconut is a bad thing (for some), but because sometimes you don't want that flavor in a dish. "Unrefined" coconut oil, on the other hand, has that coconut flavor. Refined coconut oil is also the perfect sub for ghee if you want to make a recipe entirely dairy-free.

If you want to watch your sodium intake, these substitutions are miraculous.

TYPICAL INGREDIENT	LIGHTER VERSION
Salt	Seasoned salt
	Sodium-free seasonings (such as Dash products)
Broth	Low-sodium broth
	Garlic Broth (see recipe on page 44)
Soy sauce	Coconut aminos
	Low-sodium tamari
	Low-sodium soy sauce
Worcestershire sauce	Sugar-free steak sauce

Seasoned Salt

Seasoned salt contains less sodium than iodized salt, is more flavorful, and is called for in the majority of my recipes instead of salt. I use Lawry's.

Broth

If you're familiar with my cooking, I've already let you in on the secret that cooking anything in broth versus water greatly enhances the flavor. A great way to cut down on your sodium intake is by using low-sodium broths or bouillon bases (like Better Than Bouillon).

If you really want to control the amount of sodium in your broth, make your own! (There is a great recipe for bone broth in my first book, *The Step-by-Step Instant Pot Cookbook*.) It's so easy and couldn't be more natural.

Coconut Aminos

Like ghee, a bottle of coconut aminos will quickly become one of your new best buds. Instead of tasting like coconut, it has a flavor profile closer to that of soy sauce, although not quite as salty; in fact, it has about two-thirds less sodium and adds a wonderful flavor bomb with some sweetness. Think of it as low-sodium soy sauce meets low-sugar teriyaki sauce. Plus, it's gluten-free and soy-free.

If you're allergic to coconut, you can use tamari or low-sodium soy sauce in its place. Coconut aminos can usually be found in markets in the organic section, near the coconut oil or soy sauce, and is also easily found online.

Tamari

Tamari tastes practically identical to soy sauce and typically does not contain wheat or preservatives, usually making it gluten-free. (Traditional Japanese tamari contains only water, soybeans, and salt.) That said, make sure to always check the label if gluten is a concern. Tamari can be found in markets right next to the soy sauce, or online, and also comes in low-sodium varieties, which I recommend, if using.

Worcestershire Sauce or Sugar-Free Steak Sauce

I love cooking with this ingredient I have such trouble pronouncing ("Worst-uh-sheer" seems the most popular way), but if keto or paleo is your thing, even though it's gluten-free, the sugar in it makes it noncompliant. And if you're vegan, the fish (usually anchovies) in it means it's off-limits there as well. Using a sugar-free vegan steak sauce (such as Primal Kitchen or G Hughes) will be your best substitute here!

Salt Substitutes

I never call for Dash (formerly Mrs. Dash) in this book, but if you're looking for sodium-free seasonings that provide a hint of that flavor, this brand is an excellent option.

Additionally, you'll see many recipes calling for canned tomatoes, many of which have a salt-free option. I suggest using those, as my recipes have enough seasonings to make sure the dish has flavor without adding the extra sodium.

SUGAR & SWEETENERS

These sweet substitutions to everyday sugars are a gift from the angels of sweetness themselves.

TYPICAL INGREDIENT	LIGHTER VERSION
White sugar	Monk fruit sweetener Erythritol Swerve Stevia
Brown sugar	Raw honey Pure maple syrup Agave Golden or brown monk fruit sweetener

White Sugar Substitutes

Whether you choose monk fruit (which I always do), erythritol, coconut sugar, Swerve, or stevia, these sugar substitutes contain no sugar at all but have a similar effect. It's the perfect solution for anyone who is trying to watch their sugar intake.

Brown Sugar Substitutes

Raw honey, pure maple syrup (it will state that it's pure on the bottle and is different from other maple syrups, which are loaded with bad ingredients), and agave are the perfect replacements for any recipe that calls for a brown sugar. True, they do contain sugar, but they are natural and thus better for you. For instance, pure maple syrup is loaded with antioxidants as well as nutrients like zinc, calcium, and potassium. You can also use a golden or brown monk fruit sweetener if you'd prefer.

FLOUR & STARCH

One easy way to cut down on your carb intake is by omitting all-purpose flour and starchy staples from the equation. These subs do the trick.

TYPICAL INGREDIENT	LIGHTER VERSION
All-purpose flour	Almond flour, coconut flour, and oat flour
Potato starch	Cornstarch
	Arrowroot powder
	Tapioca powder
Potatoes	Cauliflower

Almond, Coconut, and Oat Flours

Almond, coconut, and oat (and even quinoa) flours are gluten-free and have fewer carbs than all-purpose flour. That said, none of the recipes in this book rely heavily on flour; I typically call for it only as a light dusting on chicken or as a small addition to a dessert recipe. Almond and coconut flours are keto- and paleo-friendly, but be mindful they can be a bit grainy and leave their flavor mark on a dish (more on that on page 32; see "Should You Wish to Thicken a Sauce"). By the way, to save on costs, you can make your own almond, oat, and quinoa flours by blending almonds, oats, and/or quinoa in a food processor until finely pulverized, then sifting until it's a flour-like consistency.

Starches

While potato starch isn't necessarily bad for you (it's also gluten-free), those on very carb-conscious diets may not be quick to use it. That's when gluten-free, lower-carb substitutions like cornstarch, arrowroot powder (which has more fiber than cornstarch), and tapioca powder come in.

When using any of the aforementioned, make a slurry: a mixture of equal parts cold water to the powder, stirred till no lumps remain. Then stir the slurry into your sauce to thicken it up like gravy. (Like the alternative flours, more on this to come on page 32.)

Cauliflower

Cauliflower has become quite popular in recent years (it's even used as a pizza crust, for example), and it's a magnificent stand-in for potatoes, which, as wonderful as they can be, are loaded with carbs. Cauliflower cooks much more quickly than potatoes and also works well as a base for a creamy soup such as my Cream of Cauliflower (page 76).

PASTA & GRAINS

It's not that regular pasta is bad for you, it just wears its carb badge proudly without a whole bunch of nutrients. If you're trying to get a wider array of nutrients while you consume your carbs, here are some substitutions.

TYPICAL INGREDIENT	LIGHTER VERSION
Regular pasta	Whole-wheat/whole-grain pasta
	Spinach pasta
	Gluten-free pasta
	Spaghetti squash
	Zucchini noodles (zoodles)
Rice	Cauliflower rice
	Quinoa

Pasta Variations

When shopping in the pasta aisle, you'll see there's more to pasta than meets the eye. So much so that some "pasta" isn't even pasta at all, but can still satisfy a craving when you're looking to eat healthier. While some of these other "pasta" varieties may still claim carbs, they also have a dose of fiber and veggies. Some are even gluten-free, so those who have celiac can enjoy them. (But be wary of chickpea and lentil pastas. They aren't Instant Pot friendly and will turn to mush when cooked under pressure. I learned this the hard way.) The recipes in this book touch on a few pasta varieties. If you want more in-depth information on how to pressure-cook different pastas, check out the General Cooking Charts on page 54.

Spaghetti squash is a great healthy alternative to pasta. It gets its name because, once cooked, it shreds into spaghetti-like strands. Check out my recipe for Cacio e Pepe Spaghetti Squash (page 104).

While spiralized zucchini noodles, also referred to as "zoodles," are a great alternative as well, be mindful that they don't cook well in the Instant Pot. This is because zucchini releases a lot more water while cooking than most other veggies—and when cooking is accelerated under pressure, the zoodles become watery mush. Instead of trying to cook them in the cooker, I recommend tossing zoodles in some heated sauce to make them slightly springy before serving.

Cauliflower Rice

Cauliflower isn't just a good sub for potatoes, it also makes for a low-carb, grain-free rice experience. You can find cauliflower rice in the frozen section in many markets (Trader Joe's has a good one) and wholesale clubs like Costco if you want a lot, or you can make your own by tossing raw cauliflower florets into a food processor and pulsing until it's a rice-like consistency, as in my Cauliflower Rice & Broccoli Casserole (page 126).

However, I don't recommend pressure cooking cauliflower the same as you would rice, as it's not actually rice. It cooks much more quickly and doesn't need to absorb liquid to cook (unlike rice). Like zoodles, you can simply toss the riced cauliflower into heated food for a final step and it will heat it up within a few minutes. Just make sure it's thawed first—if frozen—by following the package instructions (generally zapping in the microwave).

Even if you don't generally like cauliflower in its raw, uncooked state, give it a try in this form. I promise, it's quite enjoyable, and when it's in a sauce, meat dish, or casserole, you'll very likely be fooled you're not eating actual rice.

Quinoa

Pronounced "KEEN-wah" and often classified as a grain when it is actually a seed, quinoa was first cultivated in the Andes mountains of South America. It has the slightly nutty taste of brown rice combined with a hint of oatmeal but on the fluffy, softer side. It's delightful and light and loaded with protein, making it one of the healthiest rice alternatives you can eat.

A list of all the pantry staples I strongly suggest keeping on hand follows, as spices, herbs, oils, and veggies make up a third to a half of the ingredients each recipe calls for (no fancy brands required!).

JEFF'S PANTRY STAPLES

DRIED HERBS, SPICES, AND SEASONINGS

Bay leaves

Black pepper

Cayenne pepper

Cilantro

Cinnamon, ground

Creole/Cajun/Louisiana seasoning (I like Tony Chachere's)

Crushed red pepper flakes

Cumin, both ground and seeds

Dill

Garam masala (an Indian spice blend easily found in many markets or online)

Garlic powder

Garlic salt

Italian seasoning

Kosher salt

Mustard, ground

Old Bay seasoning

Onion powder

Oregano

Paprika

Parsley

Poultry seasoning

Rosemary

Sage

Saffron (it's the most costly thing on this list, but you use only a pinch at a time)

Salt-free seasoning (such as Dash)

Seasoned salt (such as Lawry's)

Sugar substitutes (monk fruit sweetener, erythritol, stevia, or Swerve)

Thyme

Turmeric, ground

White pepper, ground

Zatarain's Concentrated Shrimp & Crab Boil

OILS, VINEGARS, SAUCES, AND OTHER PANTRY STAPLES

Agave (interchangeable with honey)

Almond, cashew, oat, or soy milk (all unsweetened)

Almond flour

Apple cider vinegar

Balsamic vinegar

Broth (chicken, beef, and/or vegetable), low-sodium

Coconut aminos, low-sodium soy sauce, or tamari

Coconut milk, unsweetened and light (you should be able to shake the can and it should sound like water—if using in a keto or paleo recipe, check the label to make sure it doesn't contain any added noncompliant ingredients)

Coconut oil, refined

Extra-virgin olive oil

Ghee (clarified butter)

Greek yogurt, plain

Hoisin sauce (gluten-free)

Honey, raw

Hot sauce

Liquid smoke (I use Wright's since it doesn't have any added soy or sugar. I prefer hickory flavor but any will do.)

Maple syrup, pure (not the other processed stuff)

Mustard (sugar-free or Dijon—I use Primal Kitchen)

Red wine (a dry one like a cabernet or pinot noir—use a cheap bottle)

Red wine vinegar

Sesame oil (either toasted or untoasted is fine)

Sherry, dry

Sour cream, low-fat

Sriracha

Steak sauce, sugar-free (Primal Kitchen and G Hughes make good ones)

Tomatoes, no-salt-added (canned crushed, diced, paste, and sauce)

White vinegar

White wine (a dry one like a chardonnay or sauvignon blanc—use a cheap bottle)

Worcestershire sauce

FRUITS & VEGETABLES

Bell peppers

Garlic (3 cloves = 1 tablespoon minced)

Ginger

Lemons

Limes

Onions (any kind can be used, but I suggest which ones I prefer in each recipe)

How to Use Your Instant Pot, in a Nutshell

Scan this with your phone to view my super helpful video!

Using your Instant Pot can seem daunting at first, but it's actually one of the easiest things you'll ever do. My first cookbook, *The Step-by-Step Instant Pot Cookbook,* went into great detail on how to get started, so I'll just give a brief recap here. If you want a more in-depth tutorial on how to get started, check out Pressure Luck Cooking's YouTube channel for the video "How to Get Started with Your Instant Pot." No matter which model you have, these simple instructions apply to all of them.

Here are the typical steps in the Instant Pot cooking process:

1. PREP YOUR INGREDIENTS. One of the best tips I can give you is to make sure all of your ingredients are out, chopped, and ready to go before cooking. This will prevent any scrambling around, especially once you've begun the sauté process. To make things extra easy, line them up in the order listed: that's the same order in which they'll be called for when you start cooking.

2. MAKE SURE THE REMOVABLE STAINLESS-STEEL LINER POT IS IN THE INSTANT POT. I know this seems like common sense, but you'd be surprised how many people forget to make sure this is the case. If you pour ingredients into the Instant Pot without the liner pot in place, you risk destroying the device.

3. TURN THE POT ON. When the Instant Pot is first plugged in (if the cord on your model is detachable, make sure it's firmly plugged into both the pot and the outlet), the display will read Off. So even though the screen is *on* and the device is now powered, the cooking element itself is *off*. Now you're ready to get started with cooking!

4. SAUTÉ. If a recipe calls for it (many do), hit the Sauté button, then Adjust the temperature to the More or High setting (which is what the recipes in this book call for most of the time). To adjust the temperature settings: if your model has an Adjust button, hit that; if it doesn't, hit the Sauté button again to adjust the temperature to either Less/Low, Normal/Medium, or More/High.

If your Instant Pot model has only buttons, once you turn it on it will say On after a few moments and begin to heat up. If it has a knob and a Start button, hit that button to begin the process. Most models give you a max time of 30 minutes to sauté before it turns off. No recipe in this book will require you to sauté for longer than that, so you can leave the default as is. If the display reads Hot, that means the pot is as hot as it can get, but there's no need to wait until that point before you start sautéing, as you'll see in my recipe instructions.

5. SWITCH FUNCTIONS. When done sautéing, hit the Keep Warm/Cancel or the Cancel button, depending on your model. Think of this as the Home button on a smartphone. This will make sure your pot is back in the Off position so you can then select a different function.

6. SECURE THE LID. The gasket (silicone ring inside the lid) is the key to the Instant Pot sealing properly. Before pressure cooking, make sure the gasket is firmly in the metal grooves or it will not come to pressure. Then, secure the lid by locking it into place. Make sure the valve is moved from the venting position to the sealing position. The Nova, Max, Duo Evo Plus, and Ultra models automatically seal the pot for you once the lid is secured, but other models require you to do this manually. Speaking of the lid, each model has a slightly different design, but they all have the same basic functions (see "The Parts of the Pressure Cooking Lid," page 27).

7. PRESSURE COOK. Depending on your model, hit either the Manual or Pressure Cook button (different from the Pressure Level button). Then, to adjust the time, use the +/− buttons to go up or down in time. Hours are on the left of the colon and minutes are to the right, so 00:08 is 8 minutes (and 8:00 is 8 hours, which you'll never use except for yogurt). On some older models it may just state the minutes. If that's the case, just 8 will be displayed, and that's 8 minutes. If you wish to change the pressure level from High to Low, you can by hitting the Pressure Level button. If Less/Normal/More is lit up as well, always leave it on Normal when pressure cooking. If your Instant Pot model has only buttons, it will say On within a few moments of turning on and begin to heat. If it has a knob and Start button, you'll need to hit that button to begin the process.

Make sure the Keep Warm button is lit as well, as this means the pot will switch to keeping your food warm once the pressure cooking cycle is complete.

When the pot is On, that means it's building pressure. Have patience. The greater the volume of ingredients in the pot, the longer it will take to come to pressure. Once there is enough steam built up inside the pot, the little metal pin in the lid will pop up, locking the lid. From there, the display will shortly begin to count down from the time you set (this will take a few more minutes and varies with the recipe and pot). When finished, the pot will read 00:00 or L0:00 depending on your model, and then will begin to count up, showing how much time has elapsed since the pressure cooking cycle was completed. This comes in handy for measuring the time if a recipe calls for a natural release. Speaking of which...

8. STEAM RELEASE. We'll use two types of releases in this book:

Quick Release. Once the pressure cooking is complete, move the valve or press the button/slide the switch to the venting position and the steam will release. Just be careful not to have your hand directly over the valve while this happens or you could get a nasty burn. When all the steam is released, the pin will drop, unlocking the lid for safe removal.

Natural release. Once the pressure cooking cycle is complete, let the pot sit, undisturbed, for the specified amount of time so the steam dissipates on its own. For example, if the recipe calls for a 5-minute natural release, do nothing until the display reads 00:05 or L0:05, depending on your model. After that, finish with a quick release. If a recipe calls for a full natural release, it means you do nothing until the pin in the lid drops and the lid can be opened. This can take anywhere from 5 to 45 minutes depending on the volume of food in the pot.

 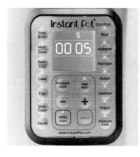

NOTE While this is unlikely to happen with my recipes, if for whatever reason the valve begins to spit out some liquid while releasing due to altitude or something else, either throw a dish towel over it or allow a full natural release. But don't allow a full natural release for pasta or rice, as they will overcook.

THE PARTS OF THE PRESSURE COOKING LID

While the lids vary by model, they all have the same functions.

A. THE VALVE. This is where you go either from venting to sealing before pressure cooking or from sealing to venting when you release the steam. On some models you have to move the valve with your finger (or a spoon if you're worried, but once you get the hang of it, it's easy to use your finger); on other models, you simply press a button or move a switch. Some models, like the Duo Evo Plus and Max, have a plastic-slotted cone that goes over the valve to help diffuse the steam while releasing.

B. THE PIN. This small metal cylinder is next to the valve. Once popped up, it serves as the gauge to show the pot is at pressure and keeps the lid locked. Once it goes back down after releasing the steam, the lid will be unlocked again. If you wish to clean the pin, remove the silicone stopper underneath it, found under the lid. Be careful not to drop it down the drain of your sink!

C. THE GROOVE. This is under the lid and holds the gasket/silicone ring. As previously mentioned, always make sure this is properly in place before pressure cooking.

D. THE ANTI-BLOCK SHIELD. This little cylinder under the lid protects any food debris from clogging up the valve while releasing. You can remove and clean it by pinching it, and then snap it back into place once cleaned.

You can also wash the lid in its entirety in the top rack of your dishwasher!

THE AIR FRYER LID

The air fryer lid is a remarkable accessory for your Instant Pot! It's essentially a convection oven packed right into the lid. The thing that makes this extra special is that you don't have to transfer your food from one pot to another to give it a final crisp after pressure cooking (like with my Crispy Carnitas, page 180). You can also use the lid as just an air fryer itself (like with my Zucchini Chips, page 243).

As of the time this book was released, there are three models of air fryer lids:

1. THE INSTANT POT AIR FRYER LID fits nearly all 6-quart models (except the Duo Evo Plus). This lid has its own attached plug that is plugged in separately from the Instant Pot. People have asked me if a separate lid for the 3- and 8-quart models will be available in the future, but only time will tell as that's up to Instant Brands to decide.

2. THE INSTANT POT DUO CRISP + AIR FRYER LID is an all-in-one 6- or 8-quart model that comes with a typical pressure cooking lid as well as an air fryer lid. Unlike the separate air fryer lid, this one powers up directly from the Instant Pot itself.

3. THE INSTANT POT PRO CRISP is a new pot, available in the 8-quart size and similar to the Duo Crisp, only sleeker and with a more generous display.

To use the air fryer lid, simply place it on top of the liner pot as you would the pressure cooking lid. If it isn't on properly, the display will read Lid. Once it beeps and says Off, it's in place. Hit any of the preset buttons you wish (I typically use Broil in my recipes, which is 400°F, the hottest it gets) and set the temperature and time using the +/– buttons. Hit Start to begin and then Cancel when done. When you hit a preset button, it automatically displays a suggested time and temperature for that setting. Depending on the setting you chose, you can still adjust the time and temperature but within specific ranges and increments. Some settings also tell you to flip the food over if you wish to do so. You can lift the lid to peek inside at any time, since it doesn't seal under pressure like the regular lid.

Regardless of which you have, all lids come with a resting disk to place the hot lid on once you're done cooking. When not using, flip the disk over and, once the air fryer lid is cooled, you can lock the open end of your lid with it for easy storing and protection of the heating element.

While some of the recipes in this book call for the option of a crispy finish with the air fryer lid (look for this icon: ♨), fear not if you don't have one! You can give it the optional finish under the broiler in your oven instead.

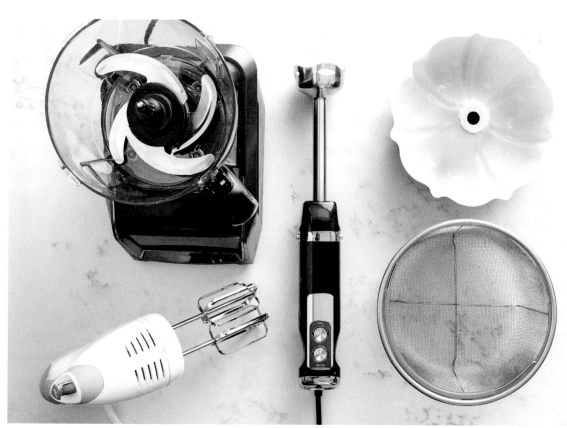

Mason Jars

A few recipes in this book, such as Ghee (page 39), Spectacular Salsa (page 46), and Mug Cakes (page 254), call for glass mason jars of various sizes. They are easily found in many markets, craft stores, and online and are cheap, pretty, reusable, and all-around fantastic things to have in your kitchen. After you make my Natural Applesauce (page 48), tie a little bow around a jar or slip a little plaid pattern under the lid, visit a neighbor or loved one, and voilà! You've just given a darling and nutritious gift! (Of course, feel free to give them a copy of this book, too. Tee-hee.)

Microplane, Cheese Grater, and Juicer

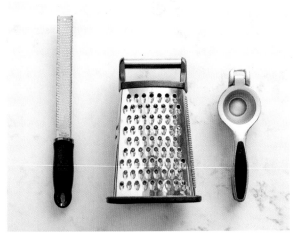

There are few things I like less than zesting a lemon or lime. Luckily, the Microplane makes it a joy. It's like a cheese grater on a violin bow and gets the job done fast and fun.

Speaking of which, don't be without a juicer and cheese grater either. They both come in mighty handy in this book.

A FEW KEY TIPS

No Liquid, No Pressure

The Instant Pot needs to have ample liquid to build steam and come to pressure. I've provided for that in all of the recipes in this book, so you shouldn't have that issue.

If Steam Is Escaping from the Sides of the Pot

It's likely the gasket/silicone ring isn't properly in the grooves under the lid. Make sure it is, but do so carefully. Also, the rings tend to wear out after about six months of regular Instant Pot use. They are easily replaced, come cheap, and can be sold in multiple colors to differentiate the types of food you're cooking, such as seafood, meats, and sweet treats (which comes in handy since they tend to retain the aromas from pungent ingredients). To help get any unwanted aromas out, wash the ring in the top rack of your dishwasher or soak overnight in vinegar and leave outside to air-dry for a day.

Deglazing

I can't stress this one enough. It's super important that while sautéing, you ensure the bottom of the pot is deglazed (scraped) with a wooden spoon to clear it of any browned bits. Again, the recipes and their instructions will remind you to deglaze as you go, so be sure to follow them as written.

Add Thick Ingredients and Most Dairy AFTER Pressure Cooking

Be sure to add most thick ingredients after pressure cooking because liquid that is too thick could tamper with the pot coming to pressure. Therefore, all cheeses and creams, if using, should be added in the final steps, just before serving. Not only are they thicker, but they can also curdle under pressure.

The Dreaded Burn Notice

If you see the word "Burn" on the screen, don't panic. Again, my recipes shouldn't lead to this notice, but if for whatever reason you encounter it, simply remove the lid (making sure any pressure is released first), give the pot a stir, and then add ½ to 1 cup more broth. From there, secure the lid again and restart the pressure cook time.

No Alcohol? No Problem.

If you don't wish to cook with wine, no problem! Simply add more broth in its place.

Hey Jeff! That's Not How My Grandma Made It!

I should hope not! She's a very special lady and I'm sure her version is untouchable in its own right. But, come to think of it, since we're pressure cooking and even air frying in some instances, nothing about this cookbook is conventional. So I make sure to bring you an array of international favorites in the best way I know how: accessibility and flavor. True, I may not use wood-ear mushrooms when a dish may traditionally feature them, but my version will give you that same authentic flavor result, no matter how unconventionally (and lightly) we achieve it.

Food Becomes Art with the Final Touches

With some recipes, the food may not look gorgeous immediately after pressure cooking and, in some cases with veggie- and protein-heavy dishes, you'll notice a lot more liquid in the pot than when you began. This is due to proteins releasing juices and veggies releasing water.

That's what the final touches are for! In recipes that can lead to excess liquid, I've instructed you to incorporate some finishing touches, such as adding a slurry to thicken the sauce or letting it rest for a few minutes for the heat to come down a bit and extra liquid to release. I promise you'll still end up with a delicious work of art!

Cooling Means Drooling

When the lid comes off the pot after pressure cooking, it's going to be *hot*. As the food rests in the pot after pressure cooking (as is the case with most soups, stews, and chilis), the longer it cools, the more the flavors come together and the more sauces, pasta, and rice thicken. This is often why leftovers can taste even better the next day after being refrigerated. After chilling out on that chilly shelf, that's when the flavors really become tight-knit.

Should You Wish to Thicken a Sauce

Many of my poultry and meat recipes make a *lot* of sauce, which I love because it can be saved and frozen for future meals or served over quinoa or cauliflower rice. And since the liquid in a pot needs to be thin enough for it to produce enough steam and fluidity for it to cook and come to pressure, a few recipes in this book call for giving a sauce a little thickening magic in the final moments before serving. This is achieved with a slurry.

Typically, we mix equal parts cornstarch or arrowroot powder (both gluten-free) with cold water and a slurry is born. We mix them together before adding to a sauce because just dumping it into the pot will make it immediately turn into a ball of gloop rather than properly meld into the sauce—it must be its own liquid before it can be added to a larger quantity of liquid. Then we stir constantly as we pour the slurry into the bubbling pot and watch it thicken up perfectly before our eyes.

I've tried making a slurry with almond flour, oat flour, and coconut flour as well, and it's just not as strong and can make a sauce quite grainy and taste like said flour. But whole-wheat flour works decently. However, if you use that, keep in mind that it has gluten, whereas cornstarch and arrowroot do not.

Now whether you follow keto or paleo and feel comfortable using a slurry is up to you, and I indicate as such in each recipe that calls for it. Cornstarch has around 30 calories and 7g of carbs per tablespoon, but I typically don't use more than 1 or 2 tablespoons for most recipes, which, when dispersed between a usual 6-serving size, is *very* minimal (about 5 calories and 1.2g of carbs per serving). Bear in mind this is also going into a sauce and you won't be lapping up every last ounce of it, so it's even more diluted. But it's totally your choice if you decide not to use it and you're fine with a thinner sauce.

Dredging Chicken

To the point above, a few poultry recipes, like Jeffrey's Favorite Chicken (page 145), begin with lightly dredging chicken cutlets in a seasoned whole-wheat flour, quinoa flour, or coconut flour mixture prior to searing for a few minutes. This just gives the chicken some proper browning and a very pleasant texture (more so with whole-wheat flour than coconut or quinoa flour). When called for, I never exceed ¼ cup.

Also, bear in mind that not all the flour may even be used, since I call for a light dusting. If a recipe states it's keto or paleo and this is also something you're not interested in, you can skip the searing of the chicken altogether and just begin by sautéing the veggies the recipe calls for. Your body, your rules.

Can These Recipes Be Made in Any Size Instant Pot?

Yes! All the recipes in this book were tested in a 6-quart model but can also be done in a 10-quart, 8-quart, or 3-quart just as well. If using a 10- or 8-quart, I usually add ½ to 1 cup more broth than called for due to the volume of the pot. Cook time remains the same. The 8-quart will also take longer to come to pressure as there's more space to fill. The opposite holds true for the 3-quart: it'll come to pressure more quickly because it's smaller, but it's also more limited as to how much it can hold. Make sure to *halve all the ingredients when using the smaller model*, but you can keep the cook time the same in most circumstances (except roasts).

If you plan on making yogurt (page 36), you can do this in any model and size *except* for the Lux, Duo Crisp, and Pro Crisp, as they simply don't offer a Yogurt setting.

How Do I Keep My Instant Pot Shiny Like the Day It Was Born?

Bar Keeper's Friend will be your and your Instant Pot's bestie.

A Few Final Thoughts

And just like that, you're ready to begin cooking!

Remember, this is a cookbook focused on lighter eating. But, as always, please feel free to add your own twist to the recipes here. It's not like I'll be peering through your kitchen window, making sure you follow everything to a T and yelling at you if you use full-fat sour cream or Boursin instead of Greek yogurt, which will of course make the food that much richer and more decadent. If you see tweaks you want to make because you either aren't a fan of a specific ingredient, don't want something spicy, or aren't able to tolerate something due to a food allergy or medical condition, by all means, swap it for something else or leave it out entirely!

Think of my recipes as a blueprint and then feel free to make them your own. Your kitchen, your body, your rules.

And now, let's eat!

—Jeffrey

1

BASICS
FOR NOW & LATER

These recipes are all incredibly easy to make
and serve as a great way to dive into Instant Pot cooking.
As delicious as they are on their own, some will also
serve as key ingredients in many of the recipes this book has
to offer. And most of them can be enjoyed right when
you make them or saved for later use.

≋ = AIR FRYER LID DF = DAIRY-FREE

K = KETO GF = GLUTEN-FREE

P = PALEO V = VEGETARIAN

+ = COMPLIANT WITH MODIFICATIONS VN = VEGAN

YOGURT TWO WAYS

If your Instant Pot has a Yogurt button on it, you're about to witness some serious magic. Not only can it make the most amazing homemade yogurt, most of the process will take place while you sleep. Yup. It's that easy. This recipe enables you to make yogurt two ways, with the Greek version used as a healthy substitute for cream in dishes like my Tofu Tikka Masala (page 224). Yogurt can *only* be made in an Instant Pot that has the Yogurt function.

Serves 13

 + *(see Jeff's Tips)*

GF

V

PER SERVING:
Calories: **58**
Fat: **2g**
Carbs: **3.1g**
Sodium: **57mg**
Protein: **6.6g**
Fiber: **0g**
Sugars: **6.6g**

Prep Time	Incubating Time	Chilling Time	Total Time
1 MINUTE	**8–10** HRS	**4–8** HRS	**12–18** HRS

THE YOGURT

1 (52-ounce) bottle 2% Fairlife milk or any *ultra-pasteurized* milk (see Jeff's Tips)

2 tablespoons plain dairy yogurt with live/active cultures (see Jeff's tips)

OPTIONAL SWEETENERS & MIX-INS

Raw honey, agave, maple syrup, or sweetener such as monk fruit or stevia

Fresh fruit, granola, and/or raw nuts

THE INCUBATING

1 Combine the milk and yogurt in the Instant Pot and whisk together.

2 Secure the lid and leave it in the venting position. (NOTE: This is the only recipe in the book that calls for the valve to be in the venting position.) Hit the Yogurt button and Adjust so it's on the Normal or Medium setting. (NOTE: It must be on this setting or it won't become proper yogurt.) The time should display 8 hours. If you want a tangier flavor, adjust the time up to 10 hours. The yogurt incubates and therefore the pot will not come to pressure.

3 Once done, the display will read Yogt. Remove the lid (remember, there won't be any quick or natural releasing as it wasn't pressure cooked).

CONTINUES

This recipe can be considered keto-friendly if you use whole Fairlife milk and strain it. This is because it's higher in protein and lower in carbs since all the whey has been strained out.

Don't try to use regular milk when making yogurt in an Instant Pot. It must be ultra-pasteurized for this recipe to work. Fairlife works great and also happens to be lactose-free and super high in protein and calcium! For a richer yogurt, use whole Fairlife. Canadians should use Natrel lactose-free milk since Fairlife may not be regularly available there.

Making yogurt is like planting seeds. Once you finish a batch, you can use 2 tablespoons as the starter for the next batch instead of opening up a new container of store-bought yogurt. Just make sure you do this within 1 week of making the yogurt so it's fresh and active for the next batch. If I don't have any homemade yogurt on hand, I use Chobani fat-free Greek yogurt. For a richer yogurt, you can use whole yogurt.

If you want your yogurt to have a smooth, creamy texture, there is no need to strain it.

1 Remove the liner pot from the Instant Pot (it won't be hot). Do not mix the yogurt. Cover the liner pot with aluminum foil and set in the fridge to chill for 4–8 hours (the longer, the better). If you stick a spoon in, it should stand up on its own.

2 When ready to serve, skim/pour off any whey (liquid) that may have collected on the surface. You can either discard the whey or save it for baking bread or some other project. Serve the yogurt as is or with your favorite sweeteners or mix-ins!

If you want your yogurt to have a super thick consistency, almost like cream cheese or sour cream, we're going to strain it and do it Greek-style.

1 Remove the liner pot from the Instant Pot (it won't be hot). Pour the yogurt through a yogurt strainer (or a colander lined with coffee filters) to allow the whey (liquid) to separate from the yogurt. This is what's going to make it super thick (and will also make a magnificent substitute for cream and a base for dips—see Tzatziki Dip, page 243).

2 Cover with a lid or aluminum foil and set it in the fridge to strain further for 4–8 hours (the longer, the better).

3 When ready to serve, you can either discard the whey or save it for baking bread or some other project. Serve the yogurt as is or with your favorite sweeteners or mix-ins, or use as called for in a recipe.

TO STORE

Transfer the yogurt to individual containers or leave it in one large container. Your container(s) must have an airtight cover so the yogurt can retain its cultured state. Yogurt will keep for up to 2 weeks in the fridge.

GHEE
(CLARIFIED BUTTER)

Makes 2 cups

PER SERVING
(1 TEASPOON)
Calories: **37**
Fat: **4.3g**
Carbs: **0g**
Sodium: **0mg**
Protein: **0g**
Fiber: **0g**
Sugars: **0g**

K P GF V

O. M. Ghee! This recipe can be done just as easily on your stovetop in a pot or Dutch oven, but (not surprisingly) I prefer to use the Instant Pot. Ghee, which originated in India, is a clarified (or anhydrous) butter, which means that it's ordinary butter with all the milk solids separated out after it melts from its solid state. Once you strain the butter and cool it in the fridge, it hardens up again and can be used for months to come. Even better, it has a high heat tolerance so it won't burn as quickly as other oils or regular butter, making it ideal for sautéing. And since all the lactose is removed, ghee is paleo-compliant.

Prep Time	Sauté Time	Total Time
1 MINUTE	7 MIN	8 MIN

1 pound *unsalted* butter (I prefer Kerrygold or another high-quality butter. Don't skimp on this, and be sure it's unsalted.)

1 Fold a piece of cheesecloth to make a double layer and place it over the mouth of a 16-ounce mason jar. Allow some slack over the lip of the jar so it forms a bit of a sunken pit for catching milk solids, then screw on the ring lid.

2 Put the butter in the Instant Pot, hit Sauté, and Adjust so it's on the Less or Low setting. Heat for 3 minutes, or until the butter is melted. You can encourage quicker melting by stirring often.

CONTINUES

3 From there, it's a watching game as we want it to get to a light golden color. To achieve this, hit Sauté twice more until you're on the More or High setting (for older models, hit Keep Warm/Cancel, hit Sauté, and Adjust so you're on the More or High setting). Stir every 15 seconds for 4–5 minutes and watch it like a hawk.

4 Once the butter is a golden color (think the sun), you can see small particles form, and the top is covered with foam, it's about to quickly change to a dark brown.

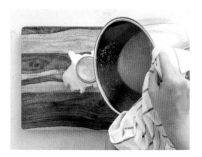

5 Immediately hit Keep Warm/Cancel and, with oven mitts or dish towels, carefully strain the ghee into the jar through the cheesecloth filter. The jar will get hot, so be careful when touching. Let the ghee cool on the counter for an hour, then remove the cheesecloth, secure the full lid, and pop it in the fridge to solidify.

6 Use the ghee as needed; it will keep in the fridge for up to 6 months.

JEFF'S TIP Pour your ghee into a silicone ice cube tray (about 1 teaspoon each) and pop in the fridge for easy use.

JEFF'S TIPS

It's perfectly normal if a few particles sink to the bottom of the jar once poured. That shows that the ghee has separated from the milk solids with success!

If it gets dark brown, you'll have brown ghee—which will be delicious as well, but will have a slightly charred flavor (like brown butter). Anything darker will taste burnt and likely unpleasant. Regardless, taste it once cooled to see if it's your style. You'll get the hang of it the more you make it, and it's a *big* money saver.

ROASTED GARLIC

Makes about 2 cups

PER SERVING (1 TEASPOON)
Calories: **12**
Fat: **0.9g**
Carbs: **1g**
Sodium: **1mg**
Protein: **0.2g**
Fiber: **0.1g**
Sugars: **0g**

If I wanted to count all the ways I use garlic, I'd need hundreds of fingers. A staple in countless recipes and a great immunity booster, this healthy gem of fragrant flavor is going to be softened, roasted, and then transformed into what can only be described as a garlic *butta* that you'll find many uses for. Schmear (that's Yiddish for "spread") it on anything you like, make my healthy Roasted Garlic & Spinach Soup (page 84), use it in mashed veggies, or even eat it on its own!

Prep Time	Pressure Building Time	Pressure Cook Time	Natural Release Time	Crisping Time	Total Time
2 MIN	5–10 MIN	5 MIN	10 MIN	12 MIN	35 MIN

4–6 large garlic bulbs, fully intact (NOTE: Bulbs are not to be confused with cloves—bulbs are made up of 10–20 cloves each.)

½–1 tablespoon extra-virgin olive oil per bulb, for drizzling

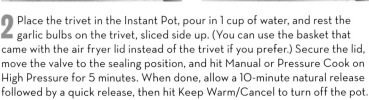

1 Using a good chef's knife, slice off the top of each garlic bulb so all the cloves are exposed.

2 Place the trivet in the Instant Pot, pour in 1 cup of water, and rest the garlic bulbs on the trivet, sliced side up. (You can use the basket that came with the air fryer lid instead of the trivet if you prefer.) Secure the lid, move the valve to the sealing position, and hit Manual or Pressure Cook on High Pressure for 5 minutes. When done, allow a 10-minute natural release followed by a quick release, then hit Keep Warm/Cancel to turn off the pot.

3 Remove the trivet and garlic bulbs, drain the liner pot, and return it to the Instant Pot, then replace the trivet or basket and garlic bulbs (still sliced side up). Drizzle the oil onto each bulb, allowing it to seep into every nook and cranny. Add the air fryer lid, hit Broil (400°F) for 12 minutes, and hit Start to begin. Check on the garlic periodically until it's roasted to your liking (it should be a rich golden brown). When done, remove the air fryer lid and let rest for 10 minutes.

4 Once cool to the touch, pull off each garlic clove and squeeze the flesh into a bowl (it will pop right out of the skin and be almost paste-like). Discard the skins (your hands will get messy from this, but that means you're doing a good job).

5 You can now do anything you want with the garlic! Store in an airtight container in the refrigerator for up to 4 days.

JEFF'S TIP If you don't have an air fryer lid, preheat your oven to 450°F with a rack in the upper third of the oven. Pressure cook the garlic bulbs as in Step 1, then place them on a foil-lined baking sheet and drizzle with the oil. Pop the sheet in the oven and roast for 5–10 minutes, until nice and browned. **(NOTE: Oven temperatures vary, so keep an eye on the garlic; mine comes out perfect after 7 minutes.)**

GARLIC BROTH

Broth is called for in the majority of recipes in this book. If you have my first cookbook (with more indulgent recipes), I have a wonderful bone broth recipe there. But one of my favorite things to use is garlic broth. In fact, I love it so much, I decided to create my own healthy version so I can carefully choose all the ingredients without compromising on flavor. It's also vegan!

Serves 8
PER SERVING
Calories: **35**
Fat: **0.2g**
Carbs: **7.7g**
Sodium: **78mg**
Protein: **1.4g**
Fiber: **1.1g**
Sugars: **1.2g**

Prep Time	Pressure Building Time	Pressure Cook Time	Total Time
5 MIN	10–15 MIN	120 MIN	2 HRS 15 MIN

40 (yes, 40!) cloves garlic, lightly smashed, or Roasted Garlic (page 42)

1 medium yellow onion, unpeeled and quartered

2 ribs celery, halved crosswise

10 whole black peppercorns

1 tablespoon garlic powder or granulated garlic

2 teaspoons garlic salt

2 sprigs thyme

2 sprigs rosemary

2 bay leaves

8 cups water

1 tablespoon apple cider vinegar

Any other seasonings you enjoy, to taste

1 Combine the garlic cloves, onion, celery, peppercorns, garlic powder, garlic salt, thyme, rosemary, and bay leaves in the Instant Pot. (NOTE: If you have a steamer basket, put the ingredients in it and lower into the pot.) Add the water and vinegar.

2 Secure the lid, move the valve to the sealing position, and hit Manual or Pressure Cook on High Pressure for 120 minutes. Quick release when done.

JEFF'S TIP Want to make it vegetable broth? Awesome! Reduce the garlic to 10 cloves and add literally any vegetables you wish (whole or scraps).

3 Carefully pour the broth through a fine-mesh strainer into a large bowl or pot; discard all the solids. (Or, if using the steamer basket, simply lift all the solids out of the liquid.) Now, taste the broth and season as you wish! The broth will keep in an airtight container in the fridge for up to 3 weeks or in the freezer for up to 3 months.

SPECTACULAR SALSA

Serves 12

PER SERVING
Calories: **86**
Fat: **3.6g**
Carbs: **12.7g**
Sodium: **302mg**
Protein: **1.8g**
Fiber: **2g**
Sugars: **8.2g**

  + *(if using monk fruit sweetener)*
 P
 DF
GF
VN

I know what you're thinking: it's unusual to cook salsa, much less *pressure cook* it. But this technique stews the veggies into the perfect texture, and infuses the entire salsa with incredible richness. Trust me, stewing salsa versus serving it raw makes a world of difference.

Prep Time	Sauté Time	Pressure Building Time	Pressure Cook Time	Natural Release Time	Chilling Time	Total Time
10 MIN	6 MIN	5–10 MIN	10 MIN	5 MIN	4–8 HRS	4½–8½ HRS

3 tablespoons extra-virgin olive oil

1 large Spanish onion *or* 2 yellow onions, diced

3 jalapeño peppers, seeded if desired and diced (optional)

6 cloves garlic, minced or pressed, or Roasted Garlic (page 42)

Juice of 1 lime

1 (28-ounce) can no-salt-added crushed tomatoes

½ cup white vinegar

½ cup Garlic Broth (page 44) or water

1 tablespoon ground cumin

1½ teaspoons seasoned salt

¼ cup chopped fresh cilantro (omit if you think it tastes like soap)

1 (14.5-ounce) can no-salt-added diced tomatoes, with their juices

1 (7-ounce) can diced green chiles, with their juices

2 tablespoons raw honey or monk fruit sweetener

1–2 tablespoons hot sauce (optional)

1 Add the oil to the Instant Pot, hit Sauté, and Adjust so it's on the More or High setting. After 3 minutes of heating, add the onion and jalapeños (if using) and sauté, stirring occasionally, for 2–3 minutes, until slightly softened. Add the garlic and sauté for 1 minute.

2 Add the lime juice and let the veggies simmer for 1 minute.

3 Add the crushed tomatoes, vinegar, broth or water, cumin, seasoned salt, and cilantro (if using). Stir until well combined. Secure the lid, move the valve to the sealing position, hit the Keep Warm/Cancel Button, and then hit Manual or Pressure Cook on High Pressure for 10 minutes. When done, allow a 5-minute natural release followed by a quick release.

4 Stir in the diced tomatoes, green chiles, honey or sweetener, and hot sauce (if using) until well combined. Allow to cool for 10 minutes, then transfer to an airtight container and let chill and meld in the fridge for 4–8 hours before serving. Store for up to 2 weeks in the fridge.

JEFF'S TIP If you want your salsa chunkier and with more crunch, stir in a diced red onion just before serving.

NATURAL APPLESAUCE

Serves 12

PER SERVING
Calories: **76**
Fat: **0g**
Carbs: **20.6g**
Sodium: **12mg**
Protein: **0g**
Fiber: **4.2g**
Sugars: **16.4g**

P
DF
GF
VN

If applesauce is just for kids, then I don't want to be a grown-up. I love this stuff. When I discovered that the Instant Pot could create a healthier version without all the extra additives and sweeteners you get in the store-bought kind? Well, let's just say I may now have a Peter Pan complex. It can also serve as an excellent sweetener in lieu of sugar, such as in my Banana Bread (page 256).

Prep Time	Pressure Building Time	Pressure Cook Time	Natural Release Time	Chilling Time	Total Time
10 MIN	5–10 MIN	5 MIN	5 MIN	4–8 HRS	4½–8½ HRS

½ cup water

½ teaspoon ground nutmeg

¼ teaspoon ground cinnamon

¼ teaspoon kosher salt

10 apples (I use 5 Granny Smith and 5 Fuji), peeled, cored, and diced (NOTE: You can leave the skin on for a darker applesauce.)

2 tablespoons pure maple syrup

1 tablespoon fresh lemon juice

1 teaspoon to 2 tablespoons raw honey or agave (optional)

1 Combine the water, nutmeg, cinnamon, and salt in the Instant Pot and mix well.

2 Add the apples and pour the maple syrup and lemon juice over them (no stirring required). Secure the lid, move the valve to the sealing position, and hit Manual or Pressure Cook on High Pressure for 5 minutes. When done, allow a 5-minute natural release followed by a quick release.

3 When you remove the lid, you'll see how much liquid the apples have released and how it's already practically an applesauce consistency. In fact, if you like your applesauce on the chunkier side, just give it a good stir and you're done! If you want it more pureed (which is how I like mine), use an immersion blender to puree it directly in the pot to the desired consistency. If you taste it in its hot state, it won't taste nearly as sweet as it will once it's cooled in the fridge, so avoid the temptation to sweeten it now.

4 Transfer the sauce to an airtight container and put it in the fridge for 4–8 hours to cool and meld. It will thicken up some, and the sweetness will really come out. If you want it even sweeter, add a bit of raw honey or agave. Store for up to 2 weeks in the fridge.

JEFF'S TIP "Only ½ cup water? I thought you needed at least 1 cup for every Instant Pot recipe!" That is an evil urban legend! The amount of added liquid depends on what you're making. Apples are already full of water, and because we have so many apples in there, as the pot comes to pressure and heats up from the ½ cup water, the apples will release a lot of their own water very quickly!

STEEL-CUT OATS

The title of this one alone makes me feel like I'm some chipper, strong fella wearing overalls, struttin' through a field. But I suppose that's fitting since these oats taste like happiness and give you a great, energetic start to the day. Feel free to add your favorite fruits or nuts to the mix and to double the recipe if you want leftovers for the rest of the week.

Serves 4

PER SERVING
Calories: **119**
Fat: **1.4g**
Carbs: **25.4g**
Sodium: **51mg**
Protein: **1.8g**
Fiber: **2.4g**
Sugars: **15.6g**

Prep Time	Pressure Building Time	Pressure Cook Time	Natural Release Time	Total Time
5 MIN	5–10 MIN	3 MIN	15 MIN	30 MIN

1 cup steel-cut oats (not the instant kind!)

2 cups water

1 cup unsweetened nondairy milk (NOTE: Do not use dairy milk, as it will scorch under pressure.)

1 apple (I use McIntosh), peeled, cored, and diced

⅛ teaspoon sea salt

1 tablespoon agave or raw honey

1 teaspoon pure maple syrup

1 teaspoon pure vanilla extract

½ teaspoon ground cinnamon

OPTIONAL TOPPINGS AND MIX-INS

Dried cranberries, fresh fruit, granola, and/or raw nuts

1 Combine the oats, water, milk, apple, and salt in the Instant Pot and mix well.

3 Stir in the agave or honey, maple syrup, vanilla, and cinnamon.

4 Serve with any toppings/mix-ins you desire.

2 Secure the lid, move the valve to the sealing position, and hit Manual or Pressure Cook on High Pressure for 3 minutes. When done, allow a 15-minute natural release followed by a quick release.

 JEFF'S TIP How sweet you want this depends on your sweet tooth that day. Feel free to add a little more agave, honey, or maple syrup to your liking, but remember that a little goes a long way.

CARROT BACON CHIPS

Serves 6

PER SERVING (ABOUT 10 CHIPS):
Calories: **114**
Fat: **0g**
Carbs: **29.2g**
Sodium: **83mg**
Protein: **0.3g**
Fiber: **0.6g**
Sugars: **24.3g**

K
P
DF
GF
VN

When I first heard about making carrot bacon, I was skeptical. But when I tried it, I realized that it isn't only a lighter substitute for a slice of that crispy crackle, but it's also vegan and fat free! You can cook this in an Instant Pot only if you have the air fryer lid—which has become a very popular and handy accessory—but if you don't have one, you can make it in your oven.

Prep Time	Crisping Time	Total Time
10 MIN	10–15 MIN	20 MIN

2 tablespoons pure maple syrup

1 tablespoon coconut aminos, low-sodium soy sauce, or tamari

2 teaspoons liquid smoke

1 teaspoon seasoned salt

1 teaspoon garlic powder

2 large carrots, peeled and sliced on the bias into ⅛-inch-thick chips (some markets sell carrot chips in the produce section)

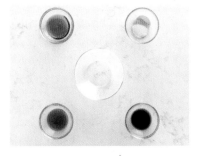

1 In a mixing bowl, whisk together the maple syrup, coconut aminos, liquid smoke, seasoned salt, and garlic powder.

JEFF'S TIPS

How crispy you like your bacon is your call and will also vary if you slice it thicker. Simply check on it while air frying and cook until it reaches the desired crispiness!

Should you wish to do this in the oven, simply place the carrot chips on a foil- or parchment paper–lined baking sheet, brush on the glaze, and bake at around 450°F for 10–15 minutes, flipping midway through, until the desired crispiness is achieved.

2 Working in batches, place the carrot chips in the air fryer basket and brush the glaze on them.

3 Add the air fryer lid, hit Broil (400°F) for 10–15 minutes, and hit Start to begin. Check on the bacon periodically until it's roasted to your liking. When done, let cool for a few moments. If desired, brush on more glaze before enjoying now or later.

GENERAL COOKING CHARTS

Here's the part where I play scientist and you get a quick reference section on how long to cook what, as well as general liquid-to-food ratios. But keep in mind that these are merely suggestions, as the dish or sauce you're making may require slightly altered ratios and times.

PASTA

PASTA	GRAIN:LIQUID RATIO BY POUND:CUP	PRESSURE COOK TIME AT HIGH PRESSURE	RELEASE
Short pasta (macaroni, rigatoni, penne, ziti, farfalle, rotini, cavatappi, cellentani, campanelle, or medium shells)	1:4	6 minutes	Quick
Linguine or egg noodles	1:4	6 minutes	Quick
Spaghetti	1:4	8 minutes	Quick
Rigatoni	1:4	8 minutes	Quick
Bucatini	1:4	12 minutes	Quick

- *If making whole-wheat pasta, cut the package's suggested minimum cook time in half, then subtract 1 minute for softer pasta or 2 minutes for al dente pasta.*
- *If making gluten-free pasta, halve the suggested Pressure Cook time in the chart above.*
- *You can't pressure cook chickpea or lentil pasta or any pasta that doesn't have a form of flour in it. It will turn to mush. Believe me, I've tried.*
- *If making pasta without a sauce, drain the excess liquid before serving.*
- *If using a long noodle such as spaghetti or linguine, you must break them in half before adding to the pot. True, some Italian grandmothers may chase you with their rolling pins for doing so, but if you don't, it won't fit or cook properly.*
- *Always add 2 tablespoons of butter/ghee or oil to the pot to prevent sticking and foaming.*

RICE & GRAINS

GRAIN (ALL RINSED FOR 90 SECONDS)	GRAIN:LIQUID RATIO BY CUP:CUP	PRESSURE COOK TIME AT HIGH PRESSURE	RELEASE
White rice (jasmine, basmati, or long-grain)	1:1	3 minutes	10-minute natural followed by quick
Brown rice*	1:1	15–25 minutes	5-10-minute natural followed by quick
Arborio rice (risotto)	1:2	6 minutes	Quick
Wild rice	1:2	25 minutes	15-minute natural followed by quick
Quinoa	1:1	1 minute	10-minute natural followed by quick
Barley	1:1½	15 minutes	10-minute natural followed by quick
Couscous (not quick-cooking)	1:2½	6 minutes	Quick
Polenta (not quick-cooking)	1:4	9 minutes	Quick
Oats (steel-cut)	1:2	3 minutes	15-minute natural followed by quick

- **For brown rice, you can go for 15 minutes with a 5-minute natural release for al dente rice or 25 minutes with a 10-minute natural release for softer rice.*
- *Cook your grains in broth instead of water to really enhance the flavor!*
- *Some people use a special rice measuring cup when measuring their rice. I don't. Use a regular measuring cup, the same as you would with liquid, for the ratios above.*

POULTRY

MEAT (2–4 POUNDS)	PRESSURE COOK TIME AT HIGH PRESSURE WITH 1 CUP OF LIQUID AND MEAT RESTING ON TRIVET	RELEASE
Chicken breasts (boneless or bone-in), 1 inch thick	12 minutes	Quick
Chicken breasts (boneless), ¼ inch thick	8 minutes	Quick
Chicken breasts (boneless), cut into bite-size pieces	5 minutes	Quick
Chicken thighs (bone-in or boneless)	8 minutes	Quick
Chicken thighs (boneless), cut into bite-size pieces	5 minutes	Quick
Chicken drumsticks	6 minutes	Quick
Chicken, whole	25 minutes	15-minute natural followed by quick
Duck breast or leg, confit	10 minutes	5-minute natural followed by quick
Duck, whole	30 minutes	15-minute natural followed by quick
Turkey, whole	40–50 minutes	12-minute natural followed by quick
Turkey breast (boneless or bone-in)	35 minutes	12-minute natural followed by quick

- All cook times are the suggested general times and will vary based on the quality, cut, and size of meat, as well as the dish you are using it in.
- For frozen cuts of meat, add 10–15 minutes of cook time. For a frozen whole chicken, duck, or turkey, thaw before cooking.

MEAT

MEAT (3–6 POUNDS)	PRESSURE COOK TIME AT HIGH PRESSURE WITH 1 CUP OF LIQUID WITH MEAT RESTING ON TRIVET	RELEASE
Beef roast (chuck, bottom, rump, round, brisket), whole	60–75 minutes	15-minute natural followed by quick
Beef roast (chuck, bottom, rump, round, brisket), cut into bite-size pieces	15–20 minutes	15-minute natural followed by quick
Beef stew meat, cut into bite-size pieces	10–18 minutes (the longer, the more tender)	5-minute natural followed by quick
Beef short ribs (boneless or bone-in)	45 minutes	15-minute natural followed by quick
Beef spare ribs (back)	30 minutes	15-minute natural followed by quick
Pork baby back ribs (back loin)	30 minutes	10-minute natural followed by quick
Pork spare ribs (St. Louis style)	30 minutes	10-minute natural followed by quick
Pork shoulder/butt	60–90 minutes	10-minute natural followed by quick
Pork tenderloin, cut into ½-inch-thick medallions	8 minutes	10-minute natural followed by quick
Pork chops (boneless or bone-in), ¾ inch thick	8 minutes	10-minute natural followed by quick
Lamb shanks	40 minutes	15-minute natural followed by quick

- All cook times are the suggested general times and will vary based on the quality, cut, and size of meat, as well as the dish you are using it in.
- For frozen cuts of meat, add 5–10 minutes of cook time. For a frozen whole roast or pork shoulder, thaw before cooking.

SEAFOOD

SEAFOOD (1–3 POUNDS)	PRESSURE COOK TIME AT HIGH PRESSURE WITH 1 CUP OF LIQUID AND SEAFOOD RESTING ON TRIVET	RELEASE
Salmon	4 minutes	Quick
Any other fish (halibut, cod, mahi, haddock, tilapia, etc.), ¼–1 inch thick	3 minutes	Quick
Large/jumbo shrimp	0 minutes	Quick
Lobster tail	4 minutes	Quick
Snow crab legs	2 minutes	Quick
King crab legs	3 minutes	Quick
Mussels, fresh	2 minutes	Quick
Clams, fresh	2 minutes	Quick

- All cook times are the suggested general times and will vary based on the quality and size of the seafood, as well as the dish you are using it in.
- If using frozen seafood, increase the Pressure Cook Time by 1 minute for shrimp and 2 minutes for all else.

BEANS & LEGUMES

1 POUND (RINSED)	PRESSURE COOK TIME AT HIGH PRESSURE, BEANS SOAKED IN SALTED WATER FOR 6–8 HOURS, THEN COOKED WITH 4 CUPS WATER OR BROTH	PRESSURE COOK TIME AT HIGH PRESSURE, BEANS UNSOAKED, COOKED WITH 4 CUPS WATER OR BROTH	RELEASE
Black beans	15–20 minutes	20–25 minutes	15-minute natural followed by quick
Black-eyed peas	10–15 minutes	30–35 minutes	15-minute natural followed by quick
Cannellini, great northern, or navy beans	10–15 minutes	35–45 minutes	15-minute natural followed by quick
Chickpea/garbanzo beans	15–20 minutes	40–45 minutes	15-minute natural followed by quick
Kidney beans	15–20 minutes	20–25 minutes	15-minute natural followed by quick
Lima beans	15–20 minutes	25–30 minutes	15-minute natural followed by quick
Pinto beans	10–15 minutes	30–35 minutes	15-minute natural followed by quick
Red beans	15–20 minutes	25–30 minutes	15-minute natural followed by quick
Lentils (brown)	N/A	10 minutes	Quick
Split peas (green or yellow)	N/A	6 minutes	15-minute natural followed by quick

- All cook times are the suggested general times and may vary based on the dish you are using the beans in.

VEGETABLES

VEGETABLE	PRESSURE COOK TIME AT HIGH PRESSURE WITH 1 CUP OF LIQUID AND VEGGIES RESTING ON TRIVET OR IN STEAMER BASKET	RELEASE
Artichokes, whole	12 minutes	Quick
Asparagus	1 minute	Quick
Beets (larger require more time)	15–25 minutes	Quick
Bell peppers, whole	3 minutes	Quick
Broccoli florets	1 minute	Quick
Brussels sprouts	2 minutes	Quick
Cabbage, whole head	8 minutes	Quick
Carrots	2 minutes	Quick
Cauliflower, whole head	4 minutes	Quick
Celery	3 minutes	Quick
Corn, on the cob	3 minutes	Quick
Eggplant, sliced	2 minutes	Quick
Green beans	3 minutes	Quick
Greens (collards, kale, spinach, etc.)	4 minutes	Quick
Okra	2 minutes	Quick
Onions, sliced	4 minutes	Quick
Peas	1 minute	Quick
Potatoes, peeled and cubed	6 minutes	Quick
Potatoes, whole	15 minutes	10-minute natural followed by quick
Squash (butternut or acorn), halved	6–10 minutes	Quick
Sweet potatoes	10–15 minutes	10-minute natural followed by quick
Tomatoes, whole	3 minutes	Quick
Zucchini, sliced	2 minutes	Quick

* All cook times are the suggested general times and may vary based on the dish you are using the vegetables in.

* If veggies are frozen, add 1–2 minutes more.

2

SOUPS & STEWS

What could be better or more comforting than
curling up with a nice, piping-hot bowl of soup to warm you
up and satisfy your appetite? The answer: knowing you've
made a healthy choice while you're slurping it. In this chapter,
I bring you simply astounding soups that are easy on the
waistline and heavy on the flavor.

= AIR FRYER LID   DF = DAIRY-FREE

K = KETO   GF = GLUTEN-FREE

P = PALEO   V = VEGETARIAN

+ = COMPLIANT WITH MODIFICATIONS   VN = VEGAN

MAGIC BEAN SOUP

While holed up in my Queens apartment during the Great Quarantine of 2020, I scoured my cupboard for basic, everyday ingredients. The challenge was to create a dish that was quick, easy, delicious, *and* healthy. The result was this soup, and it delivers on all fronts.

Serves 6

PER SERVING
Calories: **156**
Fat: **4.9g**
Carbs: **25.8g**
Sodium: **287mg**
Protein: **4.6g**
Fiber: **3.6g**
Sugars: **13.5g**

 DF + *(if using olive oil)*

GF

 VN + *(if using olive oil and vegetable broth)*

Prep Time	Sauté Time	Pressure Building Time	Pressure Cook Time	Natural Release Time	Total Time
5 MIN	7 MIN	10–15 MIN	35 MIN	20 MIN	1 HR 20 MIN

THE SOUP

- **2 tablespoons extra-virgin olive oil or ghee (store-bought or homemade, page 39)**
- **1 yellow onion, diced**
- **3 cloves garlic, minced or pressed**
- **6 cups low-sodium vegetable or chicken broth (or even water)**
- **1 pound dried great northern or cannellini beans, picked over (no need to rinse or soak!)**

SUGGESTED FLAVOR BOOSTERS

You can use any spices in your cupboard that you enjoy. I use the following:

- **2 teaspoons seasoned salt**
- **1 teaspoon black pepper**
- **1 teaspoon dried thyme**
- **1 teaspoon Italian seasoning**
- **1 tablespoon pure maple syrup**
- **½ teaspoon liquid smoke**
- **A few dashes hot sauce (I use Cholula)**

1 Add the oil or ghee to the Instant Pot, hit Sauté, and Adjust so it's on the More or High setting. After 3 minutes of heating, add the onion and sauté for 3 minutes. Add the garlic and sauté for 1 minute.

2 Pour in the broth, followed by the beans, and stir. Secure the lid, move the valve to the sealing position, hit Keep Warm/Cancel, and then hit Manual or Pressure Cook on High Pressure for 35 minutes. When done, allow a 20-minute natural release followed by a quick release.

3 Using a slotted spoon, transfer about 1 cup of the beans to a bowl. Using an immersion blender (suggested) or potato masher, puree/mash the soup in the pot. Return the reserved cup of beans to the pot and stir. (NOTE: Should you wish to have a thin soup without pureeing, simply skip this step.)

4 Add the suggested flavor boosters (or any others you prefer), stir, and serve.

JEFF'S TIP The whole point of this recipe is to serve as a base for you to play with and adjust to fit what ingredients and spices you have on hand. Missing something? Skip it or replace it. Love spices? Play around with what you have in your cupboard. Want more veggies? Add some frozen ones along with the flavor boosters in Step 4. This soup is made to be versatile!

WHITE CHICKEN CHILI

Serves 6

PER SERVING
Calories: **491**
Fat: **15.7g**
Carbs: **38g**
Sodium: **794mg**
Protein: **48.6g**
Fiber: **9.3g**
Sugars: **6.6g**

Thanks to the rousing success of the Blue Ribbon Chili from my first book, I decided to focus on its lighter cousin, White Chicken Chili, which gets its name from the absence of tomatoes. I was a little nervous to post the recipe, though: How could this one live up to the hype created by its super popular, award-winning relative? Well, because so many frustrated followers asked why I held out for so long, I'd say it was a success. I'm thrilled to finally share it in a book, where it belongs. Serve over brown rice (page 114), if you like.

Prep Time	Broiling Time	Sauté Time	Pressure Building Time	Pressure Cook Time	Total Time
10 MINUTES	**12** MIN	**10** MIN	**15–20** MIN	**5** MIN	**55** MIN

- **2 large poblano peppers, seeded and roughly chopped**
- **2 tablespoons extra-virgin olive oil**
- **2 tablespoons ghee (store-bought or homemade, page 39)**
- **1 large Spanish or yellow onion, diced**
- **3 cloves garlic, minced or pressed**
- **2½ pounds boneless, skinless chicken tenders, breasts, or thighs, cut into bite-size pieces**
- **4 cups low-sodium chicken broth**
- **1 cup salsa verde**

- **2 teaspoons ground cumin**
- **1 teaspoon chili powder**
- **1 teaspoon black pepper**
- **Juice of 1 lime**
- **1 (7-ounce) can green chiles, with their juices**
- **1 tablespoon pure maple syrup**
- **½ teaspoon liquid smoke**
- **2 (15.5-ounce) cans low-sodium cannellini, great northern, or navy beans, drained and rinsed**
- **3 tablespoons cornstarch or arrowroot powder**

- **3 tablespoons cold water**
- **1 (10-ounce) package frozen corn (optional)**
- **¼ cup plain 2% Greek yogurt (store-bought or homemade, page 36)**
- **2 teaspoons seasoned salt**
- **Shredded low-fat cheese of your choice, for garnish (optional)**
- **Chopped fresh cilantro, for garnish (optional)**

1 Scatter the poblano peppers in the Instant Pot and drizzle with the oil. Add the air fryer lid, hit Broil (400°F) for 12 minutes, and hit Start to begin. Cook until blistered. Leave the peppers and oil in the pot when done. If you don't have an air fryer lid and wish to roast the peppers first, scatter the diced poblano peppers on a foil-lined baking sheet, drizzle with the oil, and broil in the oven for 12–15 minutes, until blistered (keep an eye on them, as ovens vary). (NOTE: You can skip this step altogether if you wish, but it really brings out the flavor in the peppers, which impacts the flavor of the chili.)

2 Hit Sauté and Adjust so it's on the More or High setting. Add the ghee to the pot. Once it's melted and bubbling (about 3 minutes), add the onion (and poblano peppers and oil if you roasted the peppers in the oven or skipped Step 1). Sauté for 3 minutes, then add the garlic and sauté for 1 minute.

3 Add the chicken and sauté, stirring constantly, for another 3–4 minutes, until it turns pinkish-white (it will not be fully cooked yet, just seared).

4 Add the broth, salsa verde, cumin, chili powder, pepper, lime juice, green chiles, maple syrup, and liquid smoke and stir. Finally, add the beans on top and, rather than stirring them in, lightly smooth them out so they're just below the broth.

5 Secure the lid, move the valve to the sealing position, hit Keep Warm/Cancel, and then hit Manual or Pressure Cook on High Pressure for 5 minutes. Quick release when done.

CONTINUES

6 Mix together the cornstarch and water to form a slurry. (For a thicker chili, you may double this slurry mixture.)

7 Hit Keep Warm/Cancel followed by Sauté again. Once it begins to bubble, add the corn (if using). Stir in the slurry for 30 seconds and then hit Keep Warm/Cancel. Stir in the yogurt and seasoned salt and let set for 2 minutes.

8 Serve with a sprinkling of cheese and cilantro, if desired.

JEFF'S TIP Some people love to stir 1–2 tablespoons Chili Better Than Bouillon into the finished chili in Step 7 (I may have gotten addicted to this stuff). You can add some to your liking, but be mindful that it also increases the sodium content.

PORK POZOLE

Pozole is a deeply flavored zesty Mexican stew that features shredded pork, mild chiles, and hominy, which is simply corn kernels that have been softened in an alkaline solution. Hominy is used to make masa for corn tortillas and tamales, as well as hominy grits. Pair this soup with a cool summer night or chilly winter's day and a fresh lime juice margarita for best results. This is one of my favorite recipes of all time.

Serves 8

PER SERVING

Calories: **507**
Fat: **28.3g**
Carbs: **24.4g**
Sodium: **829mg**
Protein: **37.3g**
Fiber: **4.5g**
Sugars: **5g**

Prep Time	Sauté Time	Pressure Building Time	Pressure Cook Time	Natural Release Time	Total Time
10 MIN	10 MIN	15–20 MIN	35 MIN	15 MIN	1 HR 30 MIN

- ¼ cup extra-virgin olive oil
- 1 large Spanish or yellow onion, diced
- 1 poblano pepper, seeded and diced
- 4 jalapeño peppers, 2 seeded and diced and 2 roughly chopped with seeds and ribs intact, plus more for garnish (optional)
- 3 cloves garlic, minced or pressed
- 4 cups low-sodium beef broth or water
- 1 teaspoon liquid smoke (optional)
- 3 (15-ounce) cans white hominy, rinsed and drained

- 2 tablespoons dried oregano
- 1½ tablespoons chili powder (optional)
- 4 teaspoons seasoned salt
- 1 teaspoon ground cumin
- 1 teaspoon garlic powder
- 1 teaspoon black pepper
- ¼ teaspoon cayenne pepper (optional)
- 3 pounds boneless country-style ribs or boneless pork shoulder, cut into bite-size pieces
- 2 bay leaves

- 4 ounces dried ancho or guajillo chiles, kept whole with stems and seeds removed
- 4 cloves Roasted Garlic (page 42) or additional raw garlic
- 1 teaspoon kosher salt
- 2 (7-ounce) cans diced green chiles, with their juices

OPTIONAL TOPPINGS

Chopped fresh cilantro

Sliced radish

Lime wedges

Shredded green cabbage

Sliced jalapeños

1 Add the oil to the Instant Pot, hit Sauté, and Adjust so it's on the More or High setting. Once heated (about 3 minutes), add the onion, poblano, and the 2 diced jalapeños (if using) and sauté for 5 minutes, or until slightly softened. Add the minced garlic and sauté for 1 minute.

2 Add the broth or water, liquid smoke (if using), white hominy, oregano, chili powder (if using), seasoned salt, cumin, garlic powder, black pepper, and cayenne (if using). Stir well.

3 Add the pork, bay leaves, and ancho chiles but *do not stir*. Just make sure the chiles are smoothed out with a mixing spoon on top of everything in the pot.

CONTINUES

4 Secure the lid, move the valve to the sealing position, hit Keep Warm/Cancel, and then hit Manual or Pressure Cook on High Pressure for 35 minutes. When done, allow a 15-minute natural release followed by a quick release (the pin may have dropped on its own at this point).

5 Remove and reserve the ancho chiles, discard the bay leaves, and skim off any foam from the surface of the stew, if necessary. Transfer 2 cups of the broth from the pot to a blender or food processer and add the reserved ancho chiles, the 2 roughly chopped jalapeños (if using), roasted garlic, and kosher salt. Blend until pureed.

7 Add the diced green chiles, give everything a good stir, and let rest for 10 minutes.

8 Ladle into bowls and let everyone choose their favorite toppings.

6 Place a fine-mesh strainer over the Instant Pot and pour in the pureed chile mixture. Using some force with a wooden spoon or spatula, press the puree into the strainer, scraping it around so all the drippings drip into the pot. Do this for a good 1–2 minutes (really press all that puree through the strainer!) and then discard whatever was caught in the strainer.

JEFF'S TIPS It's common to use water instead of broth for this soup. The reason I'm giving the option of beef broth for the liquid is to give it even more flavor. Feel free to choose for yourself (as well as the flavor of broth), since the pork, hominy, and vibrant chiles are the stars of the show.

If you prefer chicken instead of pork, I'd suggest using about 3 pounds boneless, skinless thighs or breasts. Same cook time!

SPLIT PEA SOUP

Serves 6

PER SERVING
Calories: **459**
Fat: **30.8g**
Carbs: **13.2g**
Sodium: **752mg**
Protein: **31.8g**
Fiber: **4.4g**
Sugars: **2.3g**

 DF **+** *(if using olive oil)*

GF

When I was a kid, I was a bit skeptical about this one. The name is enough to make any seven-year-old giggle and the color can be … interesting. But when I grew up, I realized this soup is really just a more refined lentil soup that's been Dr. Seuss-ified with the green split peas, and it has quickly become one of my favorites!

Prep Time	Sauté Time	Pressure Building Time	Pressure Cook Time	Natural Release Time	Total Time
10 MIN	10 MIN	15–20 MIN	15 MIN	15 MIN	1 HR 5 MIN

- 3 tablespoons ghee (store-bought or homemade, page 39) or extra-virgin olive oil
- 1 yellow onion, diced
- 2 ribs celery, diced
- 1 large carrot, peeled and diced
- ½ cup dry sherry or additional broth

- 5½ cups low-sodium chicken or vegetable broth
- 1 tablespoon Worcestershire sauce or sugar-free steak sauce
- 1 teaspoon seasoned salt
- 1 teaspoon black pepper
- 1 teaspoon dried thyme
- 1 teaspoon dried oregano

- 2 bay leaves
- 1 pound dried split green peas, rinsed
- 1 ham bone or ham hock
- ¼ cup plain 2% Greek yogurt (store-bought or homemade, page 36; optional)

1 Add the ghee or olive oil to the Instant Pot and hit Sauté. Once heated (about 3 minutes), add the onion, celery, and carrot and sauté for 5 minutes, stirring occasionally.

2 Add the sherry and allow to simmer for another minute. Add the broth, Worcestershire or steak sauce, seasoned salt, pepper, thyme, oregano, bay leaves, and split peas and stir. Add the ham hock.

3 Secure the lid, move the valve to the sealing position, hit Keep Warm/Cancel, and then hit Manual or Pressure Cook on High Pressure for 15 minutes. When done, allow a 15-minute natural release followed by a quick release.

4 Discard the bay leaves and remove the ham hock (see Jeff's Tips). Stir all the contents in the pot up from the bottom as the split peas will have basically become a puree and will thicken the soup immediately once stirred up.

5 Stir in the yogurt (if using) until combined, and serve.

JEFF'S TIPS

If you want a slightly thinner soup, add another cup of broth in Step 4.

You can use some of the meat from the ham hock for garnish, if desired.

If you have leftovers, you can always save them in the fridge or even in the freezer, but note that the soup will get very thick as it cools—almost like a paste. This is because the peas continue to absorb the broth even after cooking. Once reheated, it will become soup-like again, but to achieve this, you'll have to add some more broth of your choice while reheating and mix well to thin it out a bit. Use ⅓ to ½ cup of broth for each 1 cup of leftover soup you heat up.

TURKEY TACO SOUP

Serves 6

PER SERVING
Calories: **263**
Fat: **11.4g**
Carbs: **6.5g**
Sodium: **609mg**
Protein: **36.2g**
Fiber: **1.3g**
Sugars: **2.7g**

Who says it needs to be Tuesday to enjoy tacos? And who says you need a shell to contain all those wonderful flavors? Whoever they are, you'll never listen to them again once you experience this soup fiesta that's both lighter and loaded with flavor.

Prep Time	Sauté Time	Pressure Building Time	Pressure Cook Time	Total Time
10 MIN	13 MIN	15–20 MIN	5 MIN	45 MIN

2 tablespoons extra-virgin olive oil

1 yellow onion, diced

2 jalapeño peppers, seeded if desired and diced, or 1 green bell pepper, seeded and diced

3 cloves garlic, minced or pressed

1½ pounds ground turkey or ground chicken (the leaner, the healthier)

4 cups low-sodium beef or chicken broth

Juice of 1 lime

1 (14.5-ounce) can no-salt-added diced tomatoes, with their juices

2 tablespoons hot sauce (optional)

2 tablespoons salsa verde

1 tablespoon ground cumin

2 teaspoons dried cilantro (optional)

1½ teaspoons seasoned salt

1 teaspoon chili powder (optional)

OPTIONAL TOPPINGS

Chopped fresh cilantro

A dollop of reduced-fat sour cream

Sliced avocado

Shredded low-fat cheese

Whole-wheat tortilla strips (just a few)

Sliced jalapeño

1 Add the oil to the Instant Pot, hit Sauté, and Adjust so it's on the More or High setting. After 3 minutes of heating, add the onion and peppers and sauté for 5 minutes, or until slightly softened. Add the garlic and sauté for 1 minute.

2 Add the ground turkey and sauté, breaking up the meat with a spoon, until crumbled and slightly browned, about 3 minutes.

3 Add the broth, lime juice, tomatoes, hot sauce (if using), salsa verde, cumin, dried cilantro (if using), seasoned salt, and chili powder (if using). Stir well.

4 Secure the lid, move the valve to the sealing position, hit Keep Warm/Cancel, and then hit Manual or Pressure Cook on High Pressure for 5 minutes. Quick release when done.

5 Ladle the soup into bowls and top with any desired toppings.

JEFF'S TIP This soup comes in many different varieties, but I like it with the broth on the thinner side. If you want it thicker, mix up a slurry of 3 tablespoons cornstarch or arrowroot powder plus 3 tablespoons cold water. Pour it in at the very end, bring to a simmer by hitting Sauté, then turn off the heat. It will thicken nicely.

EGG DROP SOUP

Serves 4

PER SERVING
Calories: **105**
Fat: **5g**
Carbs: **7g**
Sodium: **720mg**
Protein: **8.4g**
Fiber: **0.7g**
Sugars: **1.9g**

K + *(if okay with slurry)*
P + *(if okay with slurry)*
DF
GF
V + *(if using vegetable broth and you're okay with eggs)*

If there's one thing this Jewish guy from Long Island appreciates, it's Chinese food. It's what my family ate almost every Sunday night while I was growing up. Egg Drop Soup is an incredibly simple and light soup, yet it's also immensely satisfying and filling. This version is as easy as it gets, made with ingredients common in almost every pantry. Oh, and when those beautiful ribbons of egg form at the end? Good luck not eating it right from the pot.

Prep Time	Pressure Building Time	Pressure Cook Time	Total Time
5 MIN	10–15 MIN	3 MIN	20 MIN

- 4 cups low-sodium vegetable or chicken broth
- 1 teaspoon sesame oil
- 1 teaspoon seasoned salt
- 1 teaspoon ground ginger
- ½ teaspoon garlic powder
- ¼ teaspoon ground white pepper (optional)
- 2 tablespoons cornstarch or arrowroot powder
- 2 tablespoons cold water
- 3 scallions, chopped, plus more for optional garnish
- ¼ teaspoon ground turmeric
- 2 large eggs plus 2 large egg whites, lightly beaten

1 Combine the broth, sesame oil, seasoned salt, ginger, garlic powder, and white pepper (if using) in the Instant Pot. Secure the lid, move the valve to the sealing position, and hit Manual or Pressure Cook on High Pressure for 3 minutes. Quick release when done.

2 Mix together the cornstarch and water to form a slurry.

3 Hit Keep Warm/Cancel, hit Sauté, and Adjust so it's on the More or High setting. Add the scallions and turmeric. Once the soup begins to bubble, add the slurry and stir for another minute, until the soup has slightly thickened. Hit Keep Warm/Cancel again to turn off the pot.

4 Once the bubbles die down, pour in the beaten eggs while gently stirring with a spatula in circles so that egg ribbons form. Do this for about 1 minute, until the egg is cooked through.

5 Ladle the soup into bowls and top with additional scallions, if you desire.

JEFF'S TIPS "But, Jeff! Why are we pressure cooking just liquid and spices?" Good question! Deeper flavor infusion is part of the beauty of pressure cooking, and that's exactly what happens here when the broth and spices are brought to a rolling pressure boil in Step 1.

Some like this soup with corn to give it a sweet, complementary flavor. Feel free to add 5–10 ounces of frozen corn kernels in Step 1. And if you want to add some crunchy texture that keeps in line with tradition? Top each serving with a few chow mein noodles.

BLACK & BLUE SOUP

Serves 8

PER SERVING
Calories: **391**
Fat: **12.3g**
Carbs: **53.9g**
Sodium: **550mg**
Protein: **18.7g**
Fiber: **15.5g**
Sugars: **11.6g**

GF

V

The name of this soup doesn't lie: we're talking a classic and irresistible black bean soup served with (just a few) crumbles of blue cheese on top for an exquisite garnish. It tastes as vibrant as it looks.

Prep Time	Sauté Time	Pressure Building Time	Pressure Cook Time	Natural Release Time	Total Time
10 MIN	**8** MIN	**10–15** MIN	**40** MIN	**10** MIN	**1** HR **20** MIN

3 tablespoons extra-virgin olive oil

2 large shallots, diced

2 ribs celery, diced

1 red bell pepper, seeded and diced

6 cloves garlic, minced or pressed

6 cups low-sodium vegetable broth

Juice of 1 lime

¼ cup chopped fresh cilantro, plus more for garnish (optional)

2 teaspoons seasoned salt, divided

1 pound dried black beans, rinsed

2 bay leaves

1 tablespoon pure maple syrup

1 tablespoon ground cumin

1 teaspoon chili powder (optional)

½ cup blue cheese crumbles, for garnish

Reduced-fat sour cream, for garnish (optional)

1 Add the oil to the Instant Pot, hit Sauté, and Adjust so it's on the More or High setting. After 3 minutes of heating, add the shallots, celery, and bell pepper and sauté for 3 minutes, or until slightly softened. Add the garlic and sauté for 2 minutes.

2 Add the broth, lime juice, cilantro (if using), and 1 teaspoon of the seasoned salt. Stir well. Add the beans and stir again, then top with the bay leaves.

3 Secure the lid, move the valve to the sealing position, hit Keep Warm/Cancel, and then hit Manual or Pressure Cook on High Pressure for 40 minutes. When done, allow a 10-minute natural release followed by a quick release.

4 Discard the bay leaves. Using a slotted spoon, transfer about half of the beans to a bowl. Use an immersion blender to puree the soup in the pot until smooth.

5 Return the reserved beans to the pot and add the maple syrup, cumin, chili powder (if using), and remaining 1 teaspoon of seasoned salt. Stir until well combined.

6 Ladle into bowls and top each serving with 1 tablespoon of blue cheese crumbles, plus a sneaky drizzle of sour cream and additional fresh cilantro, if you like.

JEFF'S TIPS For a more textured soup, don't puree the soup in Step 4. Or, for a thick, totally pureed soup with no bean texture, don't remove any beans before pureeing.

If you want even more beans, in Step 5, add all or part of a (15.5-ounce) can of low-sodium black beans, drained and rinsed.

CREAM OF CAULIFLOWER

One of the things I love about soups is how easy it is to hide a bunch of healthy ingredients in a dish that tastes really indulgent. Even if you aren't a fan of cauliflower (as I once wasn't), give this one a shot. I assure you that not only will you fall in love, but this may just become your go-to soup.

Serves 6

PER SERVING
Calories: **127**
Fat: **3.6g**
Carbs: **20g**
Sodium: **350mg**
Protein: **8.3g**
Fiber: **5g**
Sugars: **10.1g**

Prep Time	Pressure Building Time	Pressure Cook Time	Total Time
10 MIN	10–15 MIN	5 MIN	25 MIN

3 cups low-sodium vegetable or chicken broth

2 medium heads cauliflower, stalks and greens removed, florets roughly chopped

6 cloves garlic or Roasted Garlic (page 42)

2 teaspoons seasoned salt

1 teaspoon black pepper

1 teaspoon garlic powder

1 teaspoon Italian seasoning

2 tablespoons ghee (store-bought or homemade, page 39); optional

2 cups unsweetened nondairy milk

1 bunch fresh chives, sliced, plus more for topping (optional)

¼ cup grated Parmesan cheese (optional)

1 Combine the broth, cauliflower florets, and garlic in the Instant Pot. Secure the lid, move the valve to the sealing position, then hit Manual or Pressure Cook on High Pressure for 5 minutes. Quick release when done.

2 Using tongs, transfer half of the cauliflower to a bowl. Use a fork to break the cauliflower into bite-size pieces (it will be very tender) and let rest.

3 Add the seasoned salt, pepper, garlic powder, and Italian seasoning to the pot. Use an immersion blender to puree the soup right in the pot.

4 Stir in the ghee (if using), milk, chives (if using), and Parmesan (if using). Add the reserved cauliflower and serve, topped with more chives, if desired.

JEFF'S TIP If you want a thick, totally pureed soup with minimal texture, don't remove any cauliflower before pureeing.

BUTTERNUT SQUASH SOUP

Nothing says autumn like this iconic soup: it tastes like a harvest in a bowl. Whether you're serving it to demanding family at the Thanksgiving table or making it for yourself, Butternut Squash Soup is rich, lush, and naturally nutritious, and will keep everyone happy.

Serves 6

PER SERVING
Calories: **200**
Fat: **8.9g**
Carbs: **27.9g**
Sodium: **717mg**
Protein: **5.1g**
Fiber: **2.2g**
Sugars: **14.8g**

 K + *(if using monk fruit sweetener)*
 P
GF
V

Prep Time	Sauté Time	Pressure Building Time	Pressure Cook Time	Total Time
5 MIN	7 MIN	15–20 MIN	8 MIN	35 MIN

1 tablespoon extra-virgin olive oil

2 tablespoons ghee (store-bought or homemade, page 39)

3 shallots, diced

3 cloves garlic, minced or pressed

4 cups low-sodium vegetable broth

1 tablespoon seasoned salt

1 teaspoon dried sage, plus more for garnish

1 teaspoon dried thyme, plus more for garnish

1 teaspoon black pepper, plus more for garnish

¼ teaspoon ground white pepper (optional)

¼ teaspoon ground nutmeg

4 cups (2 pounds) butternut squash cubes (see Jeff's Tip)

½ cup unsweetened nondairy milk

1 tablespoon pure maple syrup or monk fruit sweetener

1 tablespoon Worcestershire sauce or sugar-free steak sauce (optional)

⅓ cup grated Parmesan cheese (optional)

Pumpkin spice or ground cinnamon (optional)

1 Add the oil and ghee to the Instant Pot, hit Sauté, and Adjust so it's on the More or High setting. Once the oil's bubbling and the ghee's melted (about 3 minutes), add the shallots and sauté for 3 minutes, or until slightly softened. Add the garlic and sauté for 1 minute.

2 Add the broth, seasoned salt, sage, thyme, black pepper, white pepper (if using), and nutmeg and stir well. Add the squash and stir once more.

3 Secure the lid, move the valve to the sealing position, hit Keep Warm/Cancel, and then hit Manual or Pressure Cook on High Pressure for 8 minutes. Quick release when done.

4 Use an immersion blender to puree everything in the pot for about 30 seconds.

5 Add the milk, maple syrup or sweetener, Worcestershire or steak sauce (if using), and Parmesan (if using) and stir until well combined. For an even stronger "harvest" kick, add a sprinkle of pumpkin spice or cinnamon as well.

6 Ladle into bowls and top each serving with extra sprinkles of black pepper, sage, and thyme.

JEFF'S TIP Many markets and Costco sell squash pre-cut, but if you're starting with a whole butternut squash that you peel and cut up yourself, be sure to reserve the seeds! Spread them out on a rimmed baking sheet lined with parchment paper or aluminum foil, drizzle on a little olive oil (or mustard oil for a kick), sprinkle on some salt and pepper, and roast in the oven at 300°F for 15–20 minutes (keep an eye on them, as ovens vary). This can also be done in the Instant Pot with the air fryer lid on Broil (400°F) for 15–20 minutes. You can then sprinkle the seeds on top of the soup for a lovely additional garnish, or just enjoy them as a snack!

MANHATTAN CLAM CHOWDER

Serves 6

PER SERVING
Calories: **131**
Fat: **5.1g**
Carbs: **13.7g**
Sodium: **821mg**
Protein: **8.4g**
Fiber: **2.2g**
Sugars: **3.6g**

DF + *(if using olive oil)*

GF

New Yawk represent! This lighter, tomato-based version of a creamy New England clam chowder could cause a foodie feud with the entire city of Boston. However, each is amazing in its own right. This is definitely the healthier of the two, and it will knock your Red Sox off.

Prep Time	Sauté Time	Pressure Building Time	Pressure Cook Time	Total Time
10 MIN	8 MIN	10–15 MIN	5 MIN	35 MIN

- 2 tablespoons ghee (store-bought or homemade, page 39) or extra-virgin olive oil
- 2 large shallots, diced
- 2 ribs celery, finely chopped (with leafy tops chopped and reserved)
- 1 cup low-sodium vegetable broth

- 1 (28-ounce) can no-salt-added crushed tomatoes
- 3 (6.5-ounce) cans chopped clams, drained, juices reserved
- ½ teaspoon seasoned salt
- ½ teaspoon black pepper
- ½ teaspoon Old Bay seasoning

- ⅛–½ teaspoon Zatarain's Concentrated Shrimp & Crab Boil (optional, and a little goes a long way, so don't go above ½ teaspoon)
- 1 pound russet potatoes, peeled and diced
- Juice of ½ lemon

1 Add the ghee or olive oil to the Instant Pot, hit Sauté, and Adjust so it's on the More or High setting. Once heated (about 3 minutes), add the shallots and chopped celery ribs and sauté for about 5 minutes, until slightly softened.

2 Add the broth, crushed tomatoes, clam juice (but not the clams yet), seasoned salt, pepper, Old Bay, Zatarain's (if using), leafy celery tops, and potatoes. Stir well.

3 Secure the lid, move the valve to the sealing position, hit Keep Warm/Cancel, and then hit Manual or Pressure Cook on High Pressure for 5 minutes. Quick release when done.

 JEFF'S TIPS

Want to use fresh clams? Go for it! Just make sure you rinse them very well to remove any sand and chop them up small. You'll also need about 1½ cups of bottled clam juice.

For a lower-carb version of this chowder that's keto and paleo friendly, replace the potatoes with a small head of cauliflower, cut into bite-size pieces.

4 Stir in the clams and lemon juice and let rest for 2 minutes before serving.

MEDITERRANEAN CHICKEN STEW

This is one of my all-time favorite dishes, as it's an incredibly hearty stew loaded with protein and rich Mediterranean flavors. Traditionally, I use ground lamb, but to make this one more health-conscious, I swapped the red meat out for tender, juicy chicken thighs. Thanks to lots of veggies and spices, there's zero sacrifice when it comes to flavor.

Serves 6

PER SERVING
Calories: **419**
Fat: **14.3g**
Carbs: **39.7g**
Sodium: **926mg**
Protein: **40g**
Fiber: **6.7g**
Sugars: **15g**

DF
GF

Prep Time	Sauté Time	Pressure Building Time	Pressure Cook Time	Total Time
10 MIN	**13** MIN	**15–20** MIN	**5** MIN	**45** MIN

- 2 tablespoons extra-virgin olive oil
- 1 yellow onion, thickly sliced
- 1 red onion, thinly sliced
- 2 medium carrots, peeled and diced
- 3 cloves garlic, minced or pressed
- 2 pounds boneless, skinless chicken thighs, cut into ¼-inch strands
- 1 tablespoon paprika
- 1 tablespoon curry powder
- 2 teaspoons ground cumin
- 2 teaspoons black pepper
- 1½ teaspoons seasoned salt
- 1 teaspoon ground cinnamon

- 1 teaspoon ground turmeric
- 1 teaspoon celery salt
- 1 teaspoon Italian seasoning
- 1 teaspoon crushed red pepper flakes (optional)
- ½ teaspoon cayenne pepper (optional)
- Juice of 1 lemon
- 4 cups Garlic Broth (page 44) or low-sodium chicken broth
- 1 (14.5-ounce) can no-salt-added diced tomatoes, with their juices
- 2 (15.5-ounce) cans low-sodium chickpeas, drained and rinsed

- 2 cups shredded cabbage (a 10-ounce bag of shredded coleslaw mix in the produce section is just enough)
- 1 (6-ounce) can no-salt-added tomato paste
- 1 cup canned no-salt-added crushed tomatoes
- 1 (10-ounce) package frozen corn (optional)

OPTIONAL TOPPINGS
- Tzatziki Dip (page 243)
- Chopped fresh cilantro
- Diced kosher dill or sour pickles

1 Add the oil to the Instant Pot, hit Sauté, and Adjust so it's on the More or High setting. Once heated (about 3 minutes), add the onions and carrots and sauté for 5 minutes, or until slightly softened. Add the garlic and sauté for 1 minute.

2 Add the chicken and sauté for about 3 minutes, until it turns pinkish-white. Add the paprika, curry powder, cumin, black pepper, seasoned salt, cinnamon, turmeric, celery salt, Italian seasoning, crushed red pepper flakes (if using), and cayenne pepper (if using). Stir well.

3 Add the lemon juice and sauté for 1 more minute. Add the broth, diced tomatoes, chickpeas, and cabbage. Stir very well, scraping the bottom of the pot to deglaze.

4 Secure the lid, move the valve to the sealing position, hit Keep Warm/Cancel, and then hit Manual or Pressure Cook on High Pressure for 5 minutes. Quick release when done.

5 Add the tomato paste, crushed tomatoes, and frozen corn (if using). Stir until the tomato paste is melded into the stew, then let sit for 5 minutes.

6 Ladle into bowls and top with a dollop of tzatziki, some fresh cilantro, and a few diced pickles, if you like.

JEFF'S TIP If you use ground lamb instead of chicken thighs, the stew will be quite rich. Just know that the lamb meat will release lots of fat, so you'll want to skim it off after pressure cooking.

ROASTED GARLIC & SPINACH SOUP

Serves 6

PER SERVING
Calories: **119**
Fat: **7.3g**
Carbs: **12.1g**
Sodium: **298mg**
Protein: **5.9g**
Fiber: **2.1g**
Sugars: **2.5g**

K

P

DF + *(if using olive oil)*

GF

V

If there's a soup that's going to build up your immunity in the chilly months and help you battle nasty colds (or vampires), it's this one. Feel free to use either cauliflower or potatoes (see Jeff's Tips) to create the final, silky texture of the soup.

Prep Time	Sauté Time	Pressure Building Time	Pressure Cook Time	Total Time
5 MIN	12 MIN	15–20 MIN	5 MIN	40 MIN

2 tablespoons ghee (store-bought or homemade, page 39) or extra-virgin olive oil

1 medium yellow onion, diced

4 bulbs' worth of Roasted Garlic (page 42)

1/2 cup dry white wine (like a sauvignon blanc) or additional broth

Juice of 1/2 lemon

5 cups Garlic Broth (page 44) or low-sodium vegetable broth

1 small head cauliflower, stalk and greens removed, florets roughly chopped

1 teaspoon dried thyme

1 teaspoon garlic salt

1/2 teaspoon black pepper

1/2 cup grated Parmesan cheese (optional)

1/2 cup unsweetened nondairy milk

5–8 ounces baby spinach, chopped

1 bunch chives, sliced, for garnish (optional)

1 Add the ghee or olive oil to the Instant Pot, hit Sauté, and Adjust so it's on the More or High setting. Once heated (about 3 minutes), add the onion and sauté for 3 minutes. Add the roasted garlic and sauté for 3 minutes, until the garlic becomes a bit browned.

2 Add the wine and lemon juice and let the onion and garlic simmer for 2 minutes more.

3 Add the broth, cauliflower, thyme, garlic salt, and pepper. Secure the lid, move the valve to the sealing position, hit Keep Warm/Cancel, and then hit Manual or Pressure Cook at High Pressure for 5 minutes. Quick release when done.

4 Use an immersion blender to puree the soup right in the pot. Add the Parmesan (if using) and milk and blend once more.

5 Stir in the spinach and allow it to wilt, about 10 minutes.

6 Ladle into bowls and, if you like, feel free to add some additional cloves of roasted garlic and sprinkle on some chives.

JEFF'S TIP If you want to make this a bit more indulgent and don't mind a few extra carbs (13g), sub 1½ pounds of peeled and diced russet potatoes for the cauliflower and make the pressure cook time 8 minutes instead of 5. Or, sub heavy cream or half-and-half for the nondairy milk. It'll up the calories by about 60 and the fat by about 6g.

BORSCHT

Despite the fact that I'm of Eastern European descent, I've never enjoyed the flavor of beets (I know, sacrilegious). I've always avoided eating anything made with them, until one day when I finally forced myself to attempt this classic soup. It changed my mind forever. You could even say my heart now "beets" for borscht.

Serves 8

PER SERVING
Calories: **133**
Fat: **5.5g**
Carbs: **19.1g**
Sodium: **232mg**
Protein: **3.1g**
Fiber: **4.3g**
Sugars: **6.7g**

 DF

GF

VN + *(if using vegetable broth)*

Prep Time	Sauté Time	Pressure Building Time	Pressure Cook Time	Total Time
10 MIN	14 MIN	15–20 MIN	8 MIN	50 MIN

3 tablespoons extra-virgin olive oil, divided

2 medium beets, trimmed, peeled, and grated (NOTE: Gloves and an apron can be a great asset here to prevent dyeing your hands and clothes with beet juice. But if you get beet stains on your hands, just rub a little baking soda and warm water on them to remove the stains.)

1 medium red onion, diced

2 ribs celery, diced

1 large carrot, peeled and sliced into ¼-inch disks

9 cloves garlic, minced or pressed, or Roasted Garlic (page 42)

5 cups low-sodium vegetable or beef broth

1 (14.5-ounce) can no-salt-added diced tomatoes, with their juices

1 pound russet potatoes, peeled and diced

2 cups shredded cabbage

A small piece of scrap meat, such as a beef bone or pork neck with some meat on it (optional)

¼ cup chopped fresh dill, plus more for garnish

3 bay leaves

2 teaspoons seasoned salt

Juice of ½ lemon

1 tablespoon white vinegar

1 tablespoon red wine vinegar

Plain 2% Greek yogurt (store-bought or homemade, page 36) or reduced-fat sour cream, for topping (optional)

1 Add 1 tablespoon of the oil to the Instant Pot, hit Sauté, and Adjust so it's on the More or High setting. After 3 minutes of heating, add the beets and sauté for 8 minutes. Transfer to a bowl and set aside.

2 Add the remaining 2 tablespoons of oil as well as the onion, celery, and carrot and sauté for 2 minutes. Add the garlic and sauté for 1 minute.

3 Add the broth, tomatoes, potatoes, cabbage, meat scraps (if using), and dill. Stir well and top with the bay leaves.

4 Secure the lid, move the valve to the sealing position, hit Keep Warm/Cancel, and then hit Manual or Pressure Cook on High Pressure for 8 minutes. Quick release when done. Remove the bay leaves and meat scraps, reserving any meat you wish for garnish.

5 Return the sautéed beets to the pot, along with the seasoned salt, lemon juice, and both vinegars and give everything a good stir.

6 Ladle into bowls and top with additional dill and a dollop of yogurt or sour cream, if desired.

JEFF'S TIPS If you want to be more carb-conscious, leave out the potatoes. While the borscht is cooking, you can microwave some cauliflower and add it in Step 5 (don't cook it in the Instant Pot because it will become pure mush if pressure cooked for that long). Losing the potatoes drops the calories by about 60 and the carbs by about 15g. It will also make it paleo-friendly.

The reason we don't pressure cook the beets is because they will become overcooked and lose their color. The soup will appear dull and bland instead of vibrant and flavorful—which is essential to a wonderful borscht!

3

PASTA

I want to start off this chapter with a quick reminder that portion control is key to a healthy eating lifestyle. Therefore, I am giving you a chapter that will focus on a palette of lighter pasta dishes that are so good and done to such perfection, they'll make you want to hug your nonna. From whole-wheat pasta to noodles made of squash to the real deal, we're gonna have some tasty fun and unlock healthier pastabilities. (Besides, there's no way I'd be able to forgive myself for putting out a cookbook and not including pasta recipes.) Oh! And, if you ever wish to sub a gluten-free pasta for any listed in this chapter, just shave 2 minutes off the cooking time; all else remains the same!

= AIR FRYER LID   DF = DAIRY-FREE

K = KETO   GF = GLUTEN-FREE

P = PALEO   V = VEGETARIAN

+ = COMPLIANT WITH MODIFICATIONS   VN = VEGAN

SPINACH, GARLIC & TOMATO PASTA

Serves 6

PER SERVING
Calories: **515**
Fat: **12g**
Carbs: **63.8g**
Sodium: **405mg**
Protein: **17.7g**
Fiber: **9.3g**
Sugars: **5.3g**

DF

VN

I almost called this dish the Three Stooges because it focuses on a trio of outrageously simple, healthy, and tasty ingredients and is so easy to make, it's goofy. You may just become a permanent fan of whole-wheat pasta after this one, too.

Prep Time	Sauté Time	Pressure Building Time	Pressure Cook Time	Total Time
10 MIN	8 MIN	5–10 MIN	4 MIN	30 MIN

¼ cup extra-virgin olive oil

2 shallots, diced

15 cloves garlic, 9 minced or pressed and 6 thinly sliced

2 cups dry white wine (like a sauvignon blanc) or additional broth

2 cups Garlic Broth (page 44) or low-sodium vegetable broth

1 pound whole-wheat penne (see Jeff's Tip)

1¼ pounds cherry or grape tomatoes

8–10 ounces baby spinach

½ cup grated Parmesan cheese (optional)

1 Add the oil to the Instant Pot, hit Sauté, and Adjust so it's on the More or High setting. After 3 minutes of heating, add the shallots and sauté for 2 minutes. Add all the garlic and sauté for 3–5 minutes, until browned but not charred.

2 Pour in the wine and scrape any dark bits from the bottom of the pot. Add the broth and pasta but *do not stir*. Just smooth it out so it's mostly submerged in the broth (it's okay if some peeks above).

3 Top with the tomatoes and spinach and again, *do not stir*. (NOTE: The reason we don't stir the pot once pasta is added is so that it won't "clog up" the pot when attempting to come to pressure. It also ensures the pasta cooks evenly.)

4 Secure the lid, move the valve to the sealing position, hit Keep Warm/Cancel, and then hit Manual or Pressure Cook on High Pressure for 4 minutes. Quick release when done.

5 Stir in the Parmesan (if using), let rest for 2 minutes to slightly cool and thicken, and serve.

JEFF'S TIP If you prefer to use regular penne, up the pressure cook time from 4 to 6 minutes in Step 4. The nutrition information remains virtually the same.

LINGUINE WITH RED CLAM SAUCE

Serves 6

DF

PER SERVING
Calories: **400**
Fat: **10.9g**
Carbs: **62.4g**
Sodium: **417mg**
Protein: **11.3g**
Fiber: **3.9g**
Sugars: **5.6g**

In my first book, I released the richer companion to this dish, with clams dressed in a beautiful butter-based white sauce. This time, I've decked out the pasta in an irresistibly zesty tomato-based rendition. One thing the two dishes have in common is abundant clams in a richly flavored sauce.

Prep Time	Sauté Time	Pressure Building Time	Pressure Cook Time	Total Time
10 MIN	7 MIN	5–10 MIN	6 MIN	30 MIN

- ¼ cup extra-virgin olive oil
- 1 large shallot, diced
- 3 cloves garlic, minced or pressed
- ¼ cup dry red wine (like a cabernet) or additional broth
- 2 cups Garlic Broth (page 44) or low-sodium chicken broth
- 2 cups marinara sauce, divided (use a good-quality sauce—I like Victoria, which Costco and many markets carry)

- 3 (6.5-ounce) cans chopped clams, drained, juices reserved
- 1½ teaspoons dried oregano
- 1 teaspoon Old Bay seasoning (optional)
- ½ teaspoon crushed red pepper flakes (optional)
- ⅛ teaspoon Zatarain's Concentrated Shrimp & Crab boil concentrate (optional)
- 1 bunch basil, stems removed

- 1 pound linguine
- 10 ounces grape or cherry tomatoes
- Grated Parmesan cheese, for topping (optional)
- Freshly ground black pepper, for topping (optional)

1 Add the oil to the Instant Pot, hit Sauté, and Adjust so it's on the More or High setting. After 3 minutes of heating, add the shallot and sauté for 2 minutes, until slightly softened. Add the garlic and sauté for 1 minute. Add the wine, deglaze, and let simmer for 1 minute.

2 Add the broth, 1 cup of the marinara, the clam juice (but not the clams yet), oregano, Old Bay (if using), crushed red pepper flakes (if using), Zatarain's (if using), and basil. Stir until well combined.

3 Break the linguine in half so it fits in the pot and lay it on top of everything in a crisscross fashion, but *do not stir*. Just use a spoon to submerge it gently in the sauce (it's okay if some pieces stick above the surface). Top with the tomatoes.

4 Secure the lid, move the valve to the sealing position, hit Keep Warm/Cancel, and then hit Manual or Pressure Cook on High Pressure for 6 minutes. Quick release when done.

5 After removing the lid, don't worry if it looks a little soupy, as that will change! Stir in the clams and remaining 1 cup of marinara and let sit for about 5 minutes, stirring occasionally, until the clams have heated and the sauce has thickened.

6 Serve topped with a few sprinkles of grated Parmesan and black pepper, if desired.

JEFF'S TIP If you want your sauce a little cheesy, add ½ cup grated Parmesan in Step 5; that will add 80 calories, 6g fat, and 300g sodium.

PESTO CHICKEN FARFALLE

Serves 6

PER SERVING
Calories: **587**
Fat: **22.1g**
Carbs: **63.1g**
Sodium: **524mg**
Protein: **34.1g**
Fiber: **9.3g**
Sugars: **5.4g**

When basil is pureed with some olive oil, pine nuts, and a little Parmesan, you get pesto. It is one of the most glorious sauces on Earth—and I've discovered it also tastes fantastic when you replace the olive oil with an avocado. And when you toss it with bowtie pasta and chicken? Well, the grass just got a little greener.

Prep Time	Pressure Building Time	Pressure Cook Time	Total Time
5 MIN	**5–10** MIN	**6** MIN	**20** MIN

THE PASTA

1 pound farfalle (bowtie pasta)

2½ cups low-sodium chicken broth or Garlic Broth (page 44)

1 pound boneless, skinless chicken breasts, cut into bite-size pieces

1 (10-ounce) package frozen peas (optional)

Chopped fresh basil, for garnish (optional)

THE PESTO

1½ cups loosely packed fresh basil leaves

3 cloves garlic, lightly smashed

½ cup grated Parmesan cheese

⅓ cup extra-virgin olive oil; or 1 ripe avocado, peeled and pitted, plus 2 tablespoons cold water (see Jeff's Tips)

¼ cup pine nuts, walnuts, or pistachios

1 Add the pasta and broth to the Instant Pot but *do not stir;* just smooth out the pasta so it's mostly submerged in the broth. Top with the chicken and again, *do not stir.* (NOTE: The reason we don't stir the pot once pasta is added is so that it won't "clog up" the pot when attempting to come to pressure. It also ensures the pasta cooks evenly.)

2 Secure the lid, move the valve to the sealing position, and hit Manual or Pressure Cook on High Pressure for 6 minutes. Quick release when done.

3 Meanwhile, combine all the pesto ingredients in a food processor or blender and blend until smooth.

4 When done pressure cooking, stir in the pesto and frozen peas (if using) and mix together until well combined. The heat of the pasta will thaw the peas immediately.

5 Serve with additional fresh basil, if desired.

 Using avocado instead of olive oil makes for a healthy, creamier pesto and will make it even more calorie-friendly. You'll lose about 30 calories and 6g of fat.

To make this gluten free, use any short-form gluten-free pasta and shave the pressure cook time down to 4 minutes.

SUN-DRIED TOMATO & SHALLOT SHELLS

Serves 6

PER SERVING
Calories: **401**
Fat: **9.5g**
Carbs: **63.3g**
Sodium: **336mg**
Protein: **11.9g**
Fiber: **3.2g**
Sugars: **5g**

Shallots maybe be on the smaller side of the onion family, but they pack the most flavorful punch! What's more, they are a match made in heaven with most pasta dishes. This one is no exception, and that's why I go quite heavy on them in this recipe.

Prep Time	Sauté Time	Pressure Building Time	Pressure Cook Time	Total Time
10 MIN	15 MIN	5–10 MIN	5 MIN	40 MIN

¼ cup extra-virgin olive oil

1 (10–12-ounce) jar sun-dried tomatoes, diced, plus 2 tablespoons of the oil

6 large shallots, roughly chopped

3 cloves garlic, minced or pressed

1 bunch scallions, sliced (reserve some for garnish)

½ cup dry white wine (like a chardonnay) or additional broth

2½ cups Garlic Broth (page 44) or low-sodium vegetable broth

1 teaspoon Italian seasoning

1 pound medium shells

Fresh oregano, for garnish

1 Add the olive oil and sun-dried tomato oil (but not the tomatoes) to the Instant Pot, hit Sauté, and Adjust so it's on the More or High setting. After 3 minutes of heating, add the shallots and sauté for 10 minutes, or until browned. Reserve about ¼ cup for garnish. Add the garlic and most of the scallions and sauté for 1 minute more.

2 Pour in the wine and deglaze the bottom of the pot. Add the broth and Italian seasoning and stir. Add the pasta but *do not stir*; just smooth it out so it's mostly submerged in the broth (it's okay if some peeks above).

3 Secure the lid, move the valve to the sealing position, hit Keep Warm/Cancel, and then hit Manual or Pressure Cook on High Pressure for 5 minutes. Quick release when done.

4 Stir in the sun-dried tomatoes and let rest for 3–5 minutes to slightly cool and thicken.

5 Serve topped with fresh oregano, the reserved browned shallots, and sliced scallions.

JEFF'S TIP

If you're opting out of alcohol, add ½ cup more broth instead of wine.

SPICY LEMON SPAGHETTI

Serves 6

PER SERVING

Calories: **472**

Fat: **15.4g**

Carbs: **66.7g**

Sodium: **497mg**

Protein: **19.5g**

Fiber: **5.3g**

Sugars: **5.3g**

Ⓥ

A good lemon sauce is one of life's simple pleasures: toss it with a long noodle such as spaghetti, and that's what happiness tastes like. I love this dish spicy, but if that's not your jam, feel free to leave out the cayenne and crushed red pepper flakes.

Prep Time	Sauté Time	Pressure Building Time	Pressure Cook Time	Total Time
10 MIN	15 MIN	5–10 MIN	8 MIN	40 MIN

¼ cup extra-virgin olive oil

2 large shallots, diced

3 teaspoons ghee (store-bought or homemade, page 39), divided

1 pound baby bella mushrooms, sliced

6 cloves garlic, minced or pressed

Juice and grated zest of 2 lemons

3½ cups Garlic Broth (page 44) or low-sodium vegetable broth

1 teaspoon dried oregano

1 teaspoon dried parsley

½–1 teaspoon cayenne pepper (optional)

½–1 teaspoon crushed red pepper flakes (optional)

1 pound spaghetti

5–8 ounces baby spinach

½ cup grated Parmesan cheese

¼ cup plain 2% Greek yogurt (store-bought or homemade, page 36)

Black pepper, for serving

1 Add the oil to the Instant Pot, hit Sauté, and Adjust so it's on the More or High setting. After 3 minutes of heating, add the shallots and sauté for 2 minutes.

2 Add 2 teaspoons of the ghee. Once it's melted and bubbling, add the mushrooms and sauté, stirring often, for 5 minutes, or until softened and cooked down. The bottom of the pot will likely brown a bit at first, but once the mushrooms begin to release their juices and become a bit syrupy, you will be able to scrape the bottom of the pot clean.

3 Add the garlic and sauté for 1 minute. Add the lemon juice and allow everything to simmer for 1 minute longer.

4 Pour in the broth, oregano, parsley, cayenne (if using), and crushed red pepper flakes (if using). Stir everything together well.

5 Break the spaghetti <hides from the nonnas> and lay it on top in a crisscross fashion, but *do not stir.* Just smooth it out with a spoon or spatula so it's lightly submerged in the broth. (The top layer may be slightly above the broth as shown, but that is fine.) Top with the remaining 1 teaspoon of ghee and the spinach and, again, *do not stir!* Just let everything rest there.

6 Secure the lid, move the valve to the sealing position, hit Keep Warm/Cancel, and then hit Manual or Pressure Cook on High Pressure for 8 minutes. Quick release when done. Give everything a good stir. Don't worry if it seems like there's a lot of liquid still in the pot. This is what we want.

7 Stir in the Parmesan, yogurt, and most of the lemon zest and let rest for 3 minutes so the sauce totally comes together.

8 Serve in bowls topped with the remaining lemon zest and a few grinds of black pepper.

JEFF'S TIP Adding a bit of ghee on top of the spaghetti before cooking helps it keep from sticking. This can also be achieved with a drizzle of olive oil.

TRI-COLOR ROTINI PRIMAVERA

Serves 6

PER SERVING
Calories: **377**
Fat: **9.9g**
Carbs: **63.9g**
Sodium: **277mg**
Protein: **14.7g**
Fiber: **10.4g**
Sugars: **4.8g**

This is the lightest pasta dish in this chapter, but it's loaded with a wonderful array of vegetables, creating a beautiful dish in both taste and color. This will also serve as a delightful pasta salad if you wish to chill it and serve it later (see Jeff's Tip).

Prep Time	Sauté Time	Pressure Building Time	Pressure Cook Time	Total Time
10 MIN	10 MIN	5–10 MIN	5 MIN	35 MIN

¼ cup extra-virgin olive oil

2 large shallots, diced

1 large carrot, peeled and diced

1 red bell pepper, seeded and diced

1 orange or yellow bell pepper, seeded and diced

1 small zucchini, quartered lengthwise and cut into ¼-inch slices crosswise

9 cloves garlic, minced or pressed

Juice of 1 lemon

2½ cups Garlic Broth (page 44) or low-sodium vegetable broth

1 teaspoon Italian seasoning

1 teaspoon dried oregano

1 pound tri-color rotini

10 ounces cherry or grape tomatoes

Grated Parmesan, for topping (optional)

1 Add the oil to the Instant Pot, hit Sauté, and Adjust so it's on the More or High setting. After 3 minutes of heating, add the shallots, carrot, bell peppers, and zucchini and sauté for 5 minutes. Add the garlic and sauté for 2 minutes.

2 Pour in the lemon juice and deglaze the bottom of the pot. Add the broth, Italian seasoning, and oregano and stir. Add the pasta but *do not stir*. Just smooth it out so it's mostly submerged in the broth. Top with the tomatoes and again, *do not stir*. (NOTE: The reason we don't stir the pot once pasta is added is so that it won't "clog up" the pot when attempting to come to pressure. It also ensures the pasta cooks evenly.)

5 Serve topped with a few sprinkles of grated Parmesan, if desired.

JEFF'S TIP Should you wish to turn this into a magnificent and refreshing pasta salad, transfer the finished dish to a bowl. Add 1 cup low-fat Italian dressing (not the creamy kind) and toss to coat. Cover and refrigerate for 4 hours before serving. The dressing will add about 50 calories and 4g fat.

3 Secure the lid, move the valve to the sealing position, hit Keep Warm/Cancel, and then hit Manual or Pressure Cook on High Pressure for 5 minutes. Quick release when done.

4 Give it all a stir and let rest for 3–5 minutes to slightly cool and thicken.

CHICKEN SAUSAGE & PEPPERS PASTA

Serves 6

PER SERVING
Calories: **584**
Fat: **19.3g**
Carbs: **72.3g**
Sodium: **840mg**
Protein: **30.2g**
Fiber: **5.5g**
Sugars: **6.2g**

If you're like me and love sausage of all kinds, you'll be glad to learn that chicken sausage is delicious and a lighter alternative to the pork varieties. When we sauté it up-front along with peppers and onions, it will serve as a base for an astoundingly great pasta.

Prep Time	Sauté Time	Pressure Building Time	Pressure Cook Time	Total Time
10 MIN	12 MIN	5–10 MIN	6 MIN	35 MIN

- ¼ cup extra-virgin olive oil
- 1 large Vidalia (sweet) onion, diced
- 3 bell peppers of any color (I like to use one each red, green, and yellow), seeded and sliced lengthwise into ¼-inch strips
- 1 pound precooked chicken sausage of your choice (see Jeff's Tips), cut into ¼-inch slices
- 6 cloves garlic, minced or pressed
- ½ cup dry white wine (like a sauvignon blanc) or additional broth
- 2½ cups low-sodium chicken broth or Garlic Broth (page 44)
- 2 teaspoons paprika
- 1 teaspoon Italian seasoning
- 1 teaspoon dried oregano
- 1 teaspoon ground cumin
- 1 pound campanelle (looks like little flower trumpets) or cavatappi/cellentani (looks like little curls)
- ½ cup crumbled cotija cheese
- 1 tablespoon hot sauce (optional, I use Cholula)

1 Add the oil to the Instant Pot, hit Sauté, and Adjust so it's on the More or High setting. After 3 minutes of heating, add the onion and bell peppers and sauté for 5 minutes. Add the sausage and garlic and sauté for 2 minutes.

2 Pour in the wine and deglaze the bottom of the pot. Simmer for 2 minutes. Add the broth, paprika, Italian seasoning, oregano, and cumin and stir to combine.

3 Add the pasta but *do not stir*. Just smooth it out so it's mostly submerged in the broth (it's okay if some peeks above).

4 Secure the lid, move the valve to the sealing position, hit Keep Warm/Cancel, and then hit Manual or Pressure Cook on High Pressure for 6 minutes. Quick release when done.

5 Add the cheese and hot sauce (if using) and stir until combined. Let rest for 3–5 minutes to slightly cool and thicken before serving.

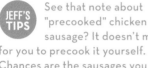

JEFF'S TIPS See that note about "precooked" chicken sausage? It doesn't mean for you to precook it yourself. Chances are the sausages you pick up in the market are precooked, as that's the norm for packaged sausages; it'll probably say it right on the package. And—bonus!—they're much easier to cut than raw sausages. But if you do get sausages that aren't precooked, just sauté the slices for 2 minutes longer in Step 1.

If you have trouble finding cotija cheese, you can use grated Parmesan or feta instead. Nutrition-wise, it's about an even trade.

To make this gluten free, use any short-form gluten-free pasta and shave the pressure cook time down to 4 minutes.

CACIO E PEPE SPAGHETTI SQUASH

This one's sort of a "fooled ya!" pasta: we use spaghetti squash in place of actual spaghetti. The result is simple and satisfying—especially since we only dress this up with some cheese ("cacio") and pepper ("pepe"). Get extra fancy by serving this delightful dish in the shell of the squash!

Serves 4

PER SERVING
Calories: **258**
Fat: **17.9g**
Carbs: **24.7g**
Sodium: **143mg**
Protein: **4.3g**
Fiber: **0.4g**
Sugars: **0g**

 K
 GF
V

Prep Time	Pressure Building Time	Pressure Cook Time	Sauté Time	Total Time
5 MIN	5-10 MIN	10 MIN	3 MIN	25 MIN

1 (3–4-pound) spaghetti squash

2 tablespoons extra-virgin olive oil

2 tablespoons ghee (store-bought or homemade, page 39)

2 tablespoons grated Parmesan cheese

2 tablespoons grated Pecorino Romano cheese or additional Parmesan

Freshly ground black pepper, to taste (freshly ground makes all the difference for this recipe)

1 Using a sharp chef's knife, slice the spaghetti squash lengthwise in half. Then scoop out the stringy, seedy center and discard. (I find an ice cream scooper works best.)

2 Place the trivet in the Instant Pot, pour in 1 cup of water, and place the squash halves on top, cut side up.

3 Secure the lid, move the valve to the sealing position, hit Keep Warm/Cancel, and then hit Manual or Pressure Cook on High Pressure for 10 minutes. Quick release when done, then hit Keep Warm/Cancel to turn off the pot.

4 Using tongs, carefully remove the squash and use a fork to shred it into spaghetti.

5 Transfer the shredded squash to a bowl and discard the squash skins (or save them to serve the finished dish in for extra "wow!" factor). Empty the liner pot, wipe it completely dry, and return it to the Instant Pot.

6 Add the oil and ghee to the Instant Pot, hit Sauté, and Adjust so it's on the More or High setting. Once the oil's bubbling and the ghee's melted (about 3 minutes), hit Keep Warm/Cancel to turn off the pot again.

7 Return the shredded spaghetti squash to the pot and toss with the ghee and oil while adding both cheeses and your desired amount of black pepper. Toss to combine.

8 Serve topped with additional black pepper.

JEFF'S TIP If you want to add some protein, such as shrimp (peeled and deveined) or bite-size pieces of boneless chicken, go for it! Add them in Step 5 and sauté until fully cooked (shrimp will curl and become opaque and chicken should be fully white, with no sign of pink).

TEQUILA-LIME SHRIMP FETTUCCINE

Serves 6

PER SERVING
Calories: **458**
Fat: **11.9g**
Carbs: **52.8g**
Sodium: **674mg**
Protein: **31g**
Fiber: **4.8g**
Sugars: **4.2g**

Most people think of a splash of white wine when they consider adding alcohol to a dish, but this one focuses instead on some sassy (and naturally low-calorie) tequila! We'll use it to dress up spinach fettuccine in a sauce that tastes so rich, you'd swear it was way more indulgent than it actually is.

Prep Time	Sauté Time	Pressure Building Time	Pressure Cook Time	Total Time
10 MIN	15 MIN	10–15 MIN	7 MIN	45 MIN

¼ cup extra-virgin olive oil

1 large shallot, diced

1 jalapeño pepper, seeded and diced (optional)

1 red bell pepper, seeded and diced

1 yellow or orange bell pepper, seeded and diced

3 cloves garlic, minced or pressed

¼ cup tequila (any kind is fine) or additional broth

Juice of 2 limes

3½ cups Garlic Broth (page 44) or low-sodium chicken broth

1 teaspoon dried oregano

1 teaspoon Cajun/Creole/Louisiana seasoning (optional, I like Tony Chachere's)

1 teaspoon Old Bay seasoning (optional)

1 teaspoon chili powder

1 pound spinach fettuccine or regular fettuccine

1 pound large shrimp, peeled and deveined

¼ cup plain 2% Greek yogurt (store-bought or homemade, page 36)

2 tablespoons chopped fresh cilantro, plus more for topping (optional)

1 Add the oil to the Instant Pot, hit Sauté, and Adjust so it's on the More or High setting. After 3 minutes of heating, add the shallot, jalapeño (if using), and bell peppers and sauté for 5 minutes. Add the garlic and sauté for 1 minute.

2 Pour in the tequila and lime juice and deglaze the bottom of the pot. Simmer for 2 minutes. Add the broth, oregano, Creole seasoning (if using), Old Bay (if using), and chili powder and stir until combined.

3 Break the pasta over the pot and, in batches, lay it in a crisscross fashion but *do not stir*. Just smooth it out so it's mostly submerged in the broth. (The top layer may be slightly a bit above the broth as shown, but that is fine.)

4 Secure the lid, move the valve to the sealing position, hit Keep Warm/Cancel, and then hit Manual or Pressure Cook on High Pressure for 7 minutes. Quick release when done.

5 Hit Keep Warm/Cancel and then Sauté again at the More or High setting. Add the shrimp and stir until curled and opaque, 3–5 minutes.

6 Add the yogurt and cilantro (if using) and stir until combined. Let rest for 3–5 minutes to slightly cool and thicken. Serve topped with more cilantro, if you like.

JEFF'S TIP Prefer chicken to shrimp? No problemo! Skip Step 5 and stir in some chopped or shredded rotisserie chicken in Step 6.

BALSAMIC MUSHROOM ORECCHIETTE

Mushrooms and balsamic are a pairing made in Italian heaven, and orecchiette pasta ("little ears" in Italian) is a perfect complement to the earthy-vinegary duo. Here, the balsamic infuses the mushrooms and seeps into the pasta, and all three come together with a slightly creamy finish to make for a meal you won't soon forget.

Serves 6

PER SERVING
Calories: **224**
Fat: **9.8g**
Carbs: **26.5g**
Sodium: **389mg**
Protein: **8.1g**
Fiber: **1.7g**
Sugars: **7.1g**

(V)

Prep Time	Sauté Time	Pressure Building Time	Pressure Cook Time	Total Time
5 MIN	12 MIN	10–15 MIN	5 MIN	35 MIN

2 tablespoons extra-virgin olive oil

2 tablespoons ghee (store-bought or homemade, page 39)

1 large shallot, diced

1 pound baby bella mushrooms, sliced

3 cloves garlic, minced or pressed

¼ cup balsamic vinegar

1 teaspoon Worcestershire sauce or sugar-free steak sauce (optional)

3¼ cups Garlic Broth (page 44) or low-sodium vegetable broth

1 teaspoon dried oregano

1 teaspoon seasoned salt

1 pound orecchiette (Frisbee-like pasta)

¼ cup plain 2% Greek yogurt (store-bought or homemade, page 36)

OPTIONAL FINISHING TOUCHES

White or black truffle oil

Balsamic glaze (see Jeff's Tips)

1 Add the oil and ghee to the Instant Pot, hit Sauté, and Adjust so it's on the More or High setting. Once the oil's bubbling and the ghee's melted (about 3 minutes), add the shallot and mushrooms. Sauté for 5 minutes, or until the mushrooms soften and begin to brown. Add the garlic and sauté for 1 minute.

2 Pour in the balsamic vinegar and Worcestershire or steak sauce (if using) and deglaze the bottom of the pot. Simmer for 3 minutes. Add the broth, oregano, and seasoned salt and stir. Add the pasta but *do not stir*; just lightly submerge in the broth with a spoon.

3 Secure the lid, move the valve to the sealing position, hit Keep Warm/Cancel, and then hit Manual or Pressure Cook on High Pressure for 5 minutes. Quick release when done.

JEFF'S TIPS

Can't find orecchiette? Use any short-form pasta. Up the cook time to 6 minutes, but if you use whole-wheat or gluten-free pasta, shave the time down to 4 minutes.

You can find balsamic glaze in small bottles next to the vinegars, oils, and salad dressings in most markets.

4 Add the yogurt and stir until melted and creamy. Let rest for 3–5 minutes to slightly cool and thicken.

5 Serve as is, or top with a drizzle of truffle oil and/or balsamic glaze.

PASTA PUTTANESCA

Serves 6

PER SERVING

Calories: **509**

Fat: **12.4g**

Carbs: **70.3g**

Sodium: **805mg**

Protein: **18.7g**

Fiber: **3g**

Sugars: **15.1g**

Puttanesca is a delightful pasta dish that features garlic, tomatoes, olives, capers, and anchovies. I know that anchovies can be a hard sell for many people, but when sautéed with shallots and garlic and then tossed with pasta, they emit a magical flavor that sets everything off beautifully. Nothing fishy about this one!

Prep Time	Sauté Time	Pressure Building Time	Pressure Cook Time	Total Time
5 MIN	7 MIN	10–15 MIN	7 MIN	30 MIN

¼ cup extra-virgin olive oil

2 large shallots, diced

5 anchovy fillets (I use flat instead of rolled), drained and chopped

6 cloves garlic, minced or pressed

3 cups Garlic Broth (page 44) or low-sodium vegetable broth

1 (28-ounce) can crushed tomatoes

2 teaspoons seasoned salt

1 teaspoon Italian seasoning

1 teaspoon dried oregano

1 pound whole-wheat spaghetti

1 tablespoon ghee (store-bought or homemade, page 39)

10 ounces cherry or grape tomatoes

1/3 cup large black or kalamata olives, pitted and sliced (optional)

2 tablespoons capers (optional)

Fresh oregano, for topping

Black pepper, for topping

1 Add the oil to the Instant Pot, hit Sauté, and Adjust so it's on the More or High setting. After 3 minutes of heating, add the shallots and anchovies. Sauté for 3 minutes, breaking apart the anchovies as you do so. Add the garlic and sauté for 1 minute.

2 Add the broth, crushed tomatoes, seasoned salt, Italian seasoning, and dried oregano and stir. Break the spaghetti in half over the pot and layer in a crisscross fashion, but *do not stir*. Just smooth it out so it's mostly submerged in the broth.

3 Top with the ghee, followed by the fresh tomatoes. Secure the lid, move the valve to the sealing position, hit Keep Warm/Cancel, and then hit Manual or Pressure Cook on High Pressure for 7 minutes. Quick release when done.

4 Add the olives (if using) and capers (if using) and stir to combine. Let rest for 1–2 minutes to slightly cool and thicken.

5 Serve topped with a sprinkle of fresh oregano and a few grinds of pepper.

JEFF'S TIPS

Want it a bit spicy? Add a few dashes of hot sauce or about ½ teaspoon crushed red pepper flakes in Step 4.

If you can't find whole-wheat spaghetti, you can use regular. Just up the cook time to 8 minutes.

4

RICE & GRAINS

Rice and grains are some of the things that the
Instant Pot does best, so naturally we have a glorious chapter
ahead. For this book, I'm focusing on the healthier
members of the grain family and dressing them up with
flavor to savor (while doing your waistline a favor). Speaking
of flavor, I always cook my rice in low-sodium broth.
But if you have only water on hand (and if you can stand to
lose a little flavor), feel free to use that instead.

= AIR FRYER LID   = DAIRY-FREE

 = KETO = GLUTEN-FREE

= PALEO = VEGETARIAN

 = COMPLIANT WITH MODIFICATIONS   = VEGAN

WHITE OR BROWN RICE

Rice is one of the quickest, easiest, and most wonderful things your Instant Pot can whip up. Here, I supply you with the two most common forms: white and brown. If you follow the recipes as written, you'll have perfect rice every time.

Serves 4

PER SERVING
White Rice/Brown Rice
Calories: **169/172**
Fat: **0.3g/1.3g**
Carbs: **37g/36.2g**
Sodium: **2mg/2mg**
Protein: **3.3g/3.6g**
Fiber: **0.6g/1.6g**
Sugars: **0.1g/0g**

 DF

 GF

VN

WHITE RICE				
Prep Time	Pressure Building Time	Pressure Cook Time	Natural Release Time	Total Time
2 MIN	5–10 MIN	3 MIN	10 MIN	25 MIN

BROWN RICE				
Prep Time	Pressure Building Time	Pressure Cook Time	Natural Release Time	Total Time
2 MIN	5–10 MIN	25 MIN	10 MIN	45 MIN

---

1 cup white or brown rice (do not use instant or Ready Rice)

1 cup water (or, for more flavor, a broth of your choice)

1 Place the rice in a fine-mesh strainer and rinse it under cold running water for about 90 seconds, shaking it around until the water coming through goes from cloudy to clear. (NOTE: Do not skip this step—unrinsed rice will be mushy and sad—unless you're making congee, page 120.)

2 Place the rinsed rice and water in the Instant Pot and stir.

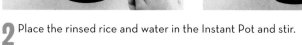

If you wish to double the recipe, go for it! Just remember to keep everything in a 1:1 ratio—meaning equal parts rice and water. The cooking and release times remain exactly the same.

3 Secure the lid, move the valve to the sealing position, and hit Manual or Pressure Cook on High Pressure for 3 minutes for white rice, 25 minutes for brown. When done, allow a 10-minute natural release followed by a quick release.

4 Remove the lid, fluff with a fork, and serve.

QUINTESSENTIAL QUINOA

Serves 6

PER SERVING
Calories: **295**
Fat: **6.3g**
Carbs: **50.5g**
Sodium: **330mg**
Protein: **11.8g**
Fiber: **8.3g**
Sugars: **3.7g**

 DF
 GF
VN

You're about to meet one of your favorite new dishes. Light, fluffy, and springy, quinoa is one of the healthiest seeds (that's often mistaken for a grain) you can eat. And when paired with Tex-Mex flavors, it'll make you want to dance. If you like, you can serve it topped with a dash of hot sauce or a small sprinkle of crumbled cotija or shredded low-fat cheese.

Prep Time	Sauté Time	Pressure Building Time	Pressure Cook Time	Natural Release Time	Total Time
5 MIN	10 MIN	10–15 MIN	1 MINUTE	10 MIN	40 MIN

3 tablespoons extra-virgin olive oil

1 small red onion, diced

1 red bell pepper, seeded and finely diced

1 jalapeño pepper, seeded and finely diced (optional)

3 cloves garlic, minced or pressed

2 cups quinoa

1½ cups low-sodium vegetable broth or Garlic Broth (page 44)

Juice of 1 lime

1 (15.5-ounce) can low-sodium black beans, with their juices

1 (14.5-ounce) can no-salt-added diced tomatoes, with their juices

½ (10-ounce) package frozen corn kernels (optional)

2 teaspoons fresh cilantro leaves, plus more for garnish (optional)

1 teaspoon ground cumin

1 teaspoon seasoned salt

1 teaspoon chili powder

Crumbled cotija cheese, grated Parmesan cheese, or nutritional yeast, for garnish (optional)

1 Add the oil to the Instant Pot, hit Sauté, and Adjust so it's on the More or High setting. After 3 minutes of heating, add the onion, bell pepper, and jalapeño (if using) and sauté for 5 minutes, until lightly softened. Add the garlic and sauté for 1 minute.

2 Meanwhile, put the quinoa in a fine-mesh strainer and rinse under cold running water for 90 seconds; drain well.

3 Add the quinoa to the pot and toss until coated in the veggies and oil.

4 Add the broth, lime juice, black beans, tomatoes, corn (if using), cilantro (if using), cumin, seasoned salt, and chili powder. Stir well.

5 Secure the lid, move the valve to the sealing position, hit Keep Warm/Cancel, and then hit Manual or Pressure Cook on High Pressure for 1 minute. When done, allow a 10-minute natural release followed by a quick release.

6 Fluff the quinoa with a fork, stir, and serve topped with additional fresh cilantro and cotija cheese, Parmesan cheese, or nutritional yeast, if desired.

JEFF'S TIP Want red kidney beans instead of black? Have at it! Calories will increase by about 30, carbs by about 7g, and protein by about 4g.

CARROT & SHALLOT "FRIED" RICE

Serves 6

PER SERVING

Calories: **327**

Fat: **10.2g**

Carbs: **54g**

Sodium: **127mg**

Protein: **5.3g**

Fiber: **2.5g**

Sugars: **1g**

DF

GF

VN

This is one of my favorite recipes in this book. Why? Because we focus on flavor-bursting shallots paired with sweet carrots! Once sautéed together, these veggies set the stage perfectly for a remarkable, light fried-style rice. I could eat this dish every day.

Prep Time	Sauté Time	Pressure Building Time	Pressure Cook Time	Natural Release Time	Total Time
5 MIN	10 MIN	10–15 MIN	25 MIN	10 MIN	1 HR

¼ cup extra-virgin olive oil

6 shallots, diced, plus more for garnish

2 large carrots, peeled and diced (about 2 cups)

6 cloves garlic, minced or pressed

2 cups brown rice (see Jeff's Tip)

2 cups low-sodium vegetable broth or Garlic Broth (page 44)

1 teaspoon seasoned salt

½ teaspoon garlic powder

½ teaspoon onion powder

2 tablespoons coconut aminos, low-sodium soy sauce, or tamari

1 tablespoon ghee (store-bought or homemade, page 39) or refined coconut oil (optional)

1 Add the oil to the Instant Pot, hit Sauté, and Adjust so it's on the More or High setting. After 3 minutes of heating, add the shallots and carrots and sauté for 5 minutes, or until lightly softened. Add the garlic and sauté for 2 minutes.

2 Meanwhile, put the rice in a fine-mesh strainer and rinse under cold running water for 90 seconds, or until the water goes from cloudy to clear; drain well.

3 Add the rice to the pot and toss until coated in the veggies and oil. Add the broth, seasoned salt, garlic powder, and onion powder and stir well.

4 Secure the lid, move the valve to the sealing position, hit Keep Warm/Cancel, and then hit Manual or Pressure Cook on High Pressure for 25 minutes. When done, allow a 10-minute natural release followed by a quick release.

5 Fluff with a fork, add the coconut aminos and the ghee or coconut oil (if using), and stir until combined. Serve topped with additional fresh shallots.

 **JEFF'S TIP** You can use just about any rice you wish for this recipe. Check the rice cooking chart on page 54 for ideas.

CHICKEN CONGEE

Serves 6

PER SERVING
Calories: **223**
Fat: **10.4g**
Carbs: **12g**
Sodium: **205mg**
Protein: **19.1g**
Fiber: **0.5g**
Sugars: **5.3g**

Congee, also known as jook and by many other names throughout Asia, is an incredibly simple and tasty Chinese rice porridge. Paired here with chicken, it is satisfying on every level—rich and thick, yet still light. Enjoy congee anytime of day: it's often served for breakfast, for warming the soul, and even as a restorative meal for those who are under the weather.

Prep Time	Pressure Building Time	Pressure Cook Time	Natural Release Time	Sauté Time	Resting Time	Total Time
5 MIN	15–20 MIN	25 MIN	20 MIN	10 MIN	20–30 MIN	1 HR 35 MIN

- **¾ cup jasmine rice (do *not* rinse)**
- **6½ cups water**
- **1 tablespoon minced or grated ginger**
- **4 cloves garlic, minced or pressed**
- **2 tablespoons pure maple syrup, divided**

- **4 pounds bone-in, skin-on chicken thighs and/or drumsticks**
- **2 teaspoons garlic salt, divided**
- **2 teaspoons seasoned salt, divided**
- **1 teaspoon garlic powder**
- **1 teaspoon onion powder**

- **¼ teaspoon ground white pepper**
- **1 tablespoon coconut aminos, low-sodium soy sauce, or tamari**
- **1 tablespoon gluten-free hoisin sauce (optional)**
- **2 teaspoons sesame oil**
- **1 bunch scallions, sliced, for topping**

1 Combine the rice, water, ginger, garlic, and 1 tablespoon of the maple syrup in the Instant Pot and stir well.

2 Add the chicken to the pot. Secure the lid, move the valve to the sealing position and hit Manual or Pressure Cook on High Pressure for 25 minutes. When done, allow a 20-minute natural release followed by a quick release. (NOTE: If this spurts a bit as it quick releases, you can either allow a full natural release or throw a dish towel over the nozzle as it releases.)

3 When the lid comes off, the congee will appear very soupy. Using tongs, transfer the chicken to a bowl to cool.

4 Hit Keep Warm/Cancel, hit Sauté, and Adjust so it's on the More or High setting. As the pot begins to bubble, add 1 teaspoon of the garlic salt and 1 teaspoon of the seasoned salt. Stir occasionally as it thickens. Once it's the desired thickness, like a thinner rice pudding (about 10 minutes), it's done.

5 Meanwhile, once the chicken's cooled, pick the meat from the bones and shred or chop it. Discard the bones, skin, and cartilage.

6 Return the chicken to the pot, along with the remaining 1 tablespoon of maple syrup, remaining 1 teaspoon of garlic salt, remaining 1 teaspoon of seasoned salt, the garlic powder, onion powder, white pepper, coconut aminos, hoisin sauce (if using), and sesame oil. Stir well.

7 Hit Keep Warm/Cancel so it's on the Keep Warm setting. And now is the time for you to have patience (and it makes all the difference with this dish). Wait 20–30 minutes for the congee to cool down significantly and thicken a bit more. This is when all the flavors come together.

8 Serve topped with sliced scallions.

 JEFF'S TIPS Jasmine rice is preferred, but if you don't have or can't find it, use long-grain white rice instead. Cook time remains the same.

This dish is also delicious cold!

GREEK FARRO FETA SALAD

Serves 6

PER SERVING
Calories: **229**
Fat: **10.8g**
Carbs: **25.9g**
Sodium: **503mg**
Protein: **7.7g**
Fiber: **4.1g**
Sugars: **2.5g**

Ⓥ

Farro is very similar to a barley and is very high in calcium, fiber, and iron. It's quite tasty, has a terrific bite, and is even more stunning when we give it a cool Mediterranean touch. This is a Greek salad fit for Zeus and Hera themselves.

Prep Time	Pressure Building Time	Pressure Cook Time	Natural Release Time	Chilling Time	Total Time
5 MIN	5–10 MIN	15 MIN	10 MIN	1 HR	1 HR 35 MIN

1½ cups farro

2½ cups water

1 small red onion, diced

1 small cucumber, skin-on and diced

1 large tomato, diced

1 (15.5-ounce) can low-sodium chickpeas, drained and rinsed

½ cup kalamata olives, pitted and chopped

⅓ cup crumbled low-fat feta cheese, plus more for garnish

¼ cup chopped fresh dill, plus more for garnish

2 tablespoons extra-virgin olive oil

2 tablespoons red wine vinegar

1 Put the farro in a fine-mesh strainer and rinse under cold running water for 90 seconds; drain well. Add the farro to the Instant Pot, along with the water.

2 Secure the lid, move the valve to the sealing position, hit Keep Warm/Cancel, and then hit Manual or Pressure Cook on High Pressure for 15 minutes. When done, allow a 10-minute natural release followed by a quick release.

3 Remove the liner pot and transfer the farro to a bowl. Cover and refrigerate for 1 hour to chill.

4 When ready to serve, add all the remaining ingredients and toss well. Serve topped with additional feta and dill, if desired.

JEFF'S TIP The sky's the limit on the veggie situation here. Add or alter however you wish!

CRISPY KALE RICE

Serves 6

PER SERVING
Calories: **387**
Fat: **15.6g**
Carbs: **56.7g**
Sodium: **192mg**
Protein: **6.5g**
Fiber: **2.9g**
Sugars: **3.4g**

Rice is an incredibly versatile base for any dish, but do you know what makes it even more exciting? When you give it a bit of a crisp. Here, sautéed kale will serve as the perfectly textured companion to this simple yet flavorful dish. Coconut aminos are a great low-sodium, gluten-free alternative to soy sauce, and provide a slightly sweeter flavor.

Prep Time	Pressure Building Time	Pressure Cook Time	Natural Release Time	Sauté Time	Total Time
10 MIN	5–10 MIN	25 MIN	10 MIN	15 MIN	1 HR

2 cups brown rice

2 cups Garlic Broth (page 44) or low-sodium vegetable broth

2 tablespoons ghee (store-bought or homemade, page 39)

4 cups stemmed and finely chopped kale (see Jeff's Tip)

2 tablespoons extra-virgin olive oil

1 shallot, diced

6 cloves garlic, minced or pressed

3 scallions, sliced, plus more for garnish

8 ounces baby bella mushrooms, sliced (optional)

2 tablespoons coconut aminos, low-sodium soy sauce, or tamari

1 tablespoon sesame oil

1 tablespoon raw honey

2 teaspoons fish sauce (optional)

Sesame seeds, for topping (optional)

1 Put the rice in a fine-mesh strainer and rinse under cold running water for 90 seconds, or until the water goes from cloudy to clear. Add the rice and broth to the Instant Pot and stir.

2 Secure the lid, move the valve to the sealing position, hit Keep Warm/Cancel, and then hit Manual or Pressure Cook on High Pressure for 25 minutes. When done, allow a 10-minute natural release followed by a quick release. Hit Keep Warm/Cancel to turn the pot off. Transfer the rice to a bowl, fluff with a fork, and set aside.

3 Add the ghee to the Instant Pot, hit Sauté, and Adjust so it's on the More or High setting. After 3 minutes of heating, add the kale and sauté for 3–5 minutes, until crispy, then use tongs or a slotted spoon to transfer to a bowl. (Don't worry if any excess kale is stuck to the bottom of the pot.)

4 Add the olive oil to the Instant Pot and let heat for 1 minute. Add the shallot, garlic, and scallions and sauté for 2 minutes. Add the mushrooms (if using) and sauté for another 3 minutes, or until slightly cooked down. Hit Keep Warm/Cancel to turn off the pot.

5 Return the rice to the pot, top with the coconut aminos, sesame oil, honey, and fish sauce (if using), and stir until combined. Add the crispy kale, reserving some for garnish, and give it a final toss.

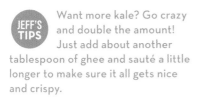

6 Serve topped with the reserved crispy kale, additional scallions, and sesame seeds, if desired.

JEFF'S TIPS Want more kale? Go crazy and double the amount! Just add about another tablespoon of ghee and sauté a little longer to make sure it all gets nice and crispy.

Some people love their rice with egg mixed in. Feel free to scramble one or two eggs in the pot when adding the mushrooms in Step 4.

CAULIFLOWER RICE & BROCCOLI CASSEROLE

If a cheesy broccoli and rice dish is your jam, enjoy it with riced cauliflower instead. By doing so, you cut the carbs way down and welcome the keto train to town.

Serves 6

PER SERVING
Calories: **213**
Fat: **13g**
Carbs: **13.2g**
Sodium: **298mg**
Protein: **13.8g**
Fiber: **5.2g**
Sugars: **5.1g**

Prep Time	Pressure Building Time	Pressure Cook Time	Sauté Time	Crisping Time	Total Time
5 MIN	5–10 MIN	1 MINUTE	8 MIN	3 MIN	25 MIN

1 large head cauliflower, stalks and greens removed, florets coarsely chopped

2 tablespoons extra-virgin olive oil

1 shallot, diced

2 cloves garlic, minced or pressed

2 cups chopped broccoli (if frozen, just put it in a bowl with ¼ cup water, cover, and microwave for 2 minutes, then drain and pat dry)

2 tablespoons ghee (store-bought or homemade, page 39)

1½ cups shredded low-fat Cheddar cheese, divided

¼ cup low-fat sour cream

1 Put the cauliflower florets in a food processor and pulse until riced. Transfer to a steamer basket.

2 Place the trivet in the Instant Pot, pour in 1 cup of water, and lower the steamer basket onto the trivet (this is so the riced cauliflower won't soak in the water directly while cooking, potentially making it soggy).

3 Secure the lid, move the valve to the sealing position, and then hit Manual or Pressure Cook on High Pressure for 1 minute. Quick release when done. Hit Keep Warm/Cancel to turn the pot off.

4 Remove the trivet and steamer basket with the cauliflower rice. Drain the liner pot, wipe it completely dry, and return it to the Instant Pot.

5 Add the oil to the pot, hit Sauté, and Adjust so it's on the More or High setting. After 3 minutes of heating, add the shallot and garlic and sauté for 2 minutes, or until slightly softened.

6 Return the cauliflower rice to the pot, add the broccoli and ghee, and sauté for 3 minutes.

7 Stir in 1 cup of the cheese and the sour cream. Once melted, hit Keep Warm/Cancel to turn off the pot.

8 Sprinkle the remaining ½ cup of cheese over the rice mixture. Add the air fryer lid, hit Broil (400°F) for 3 minutes, and hit Start to begin. When done, the cheese should be golden brown. (NOTE: If you wish to use the oven, transfer the cauliflower mixture to a small casserole dish, sprinkle with the remaining ½ cup of cheese, and broil for 2–4 minutes, until the cheese is browned. Keep an eye on it, as ovens vary.)

JEFF'S TIPS Feel free to use any kind of low-fat cheese you wish. It definitely doesn't need to be Cheddar!

You can make this dairy-free and vegan by omitting the ghee and sour cream and using vegan-friendly cheese.

SESAME-PEANUT QUINOA SALAD

Serves 8

PER SERVING
Calories: **336**
Fat: **16.1g**
Carbs: **36.7g**
Sodium: **31mg**
Protein: **12.8g**
Fiber: **5.8g**
Sugars: **2.8g**

DF
GF
VN

I was originally going to put only one quinoa recipe in this book, but it's so friggin' good, quick, and healthy, I just had to do another favorite dish. This one has flavors inspired by Thai-style peanut noodles, but with the amazing nutritional profile of quinoa. One bite and it will become a go-to side for entertaining, dinner, and anything in between.

Prep Time	Pressure Building Time	Pressure Cook Time	Natural Release Time	Chilling Time	Total Time
10 MIN	10–15 MIN	1 MINUTE	10 MIN	2 HRS	2½ HRS

2 cups quinoa

2 cups water

1 (10-ounce) bag shredded coleslaw mix (if possible, it should have red cabbage, green cabbage, and carrots)

1 red bell pepper, seeded and diced

¼ cup tightly packed chopped fresh cilantro (optional)

1 bunch scallions, thinly sliced

½ cup natural smooth peanut butter

¼ cup coconut aminos, low-sodium soy sauce, or tamari

Juice of 1 lime

1½ tablespoons sesame oil

1 tablespoon rice wine vinegar or apple cider vinegar

1 tablespoon minced or grated ginger

⅓ cup unsalted peanuts, crushed, for topping

1 tablespoon sesame seeds, for topping

Pinch crushed red pepper flakes, for topping (optional, for spice)

1 Put the quinoa in a fine-mesh strainer and rinse under cold running water for 90 seconds; drain well. Add the quinoa and water to the Instant Pot and stir.

2 Secure the lid, move the valve to the sealing position, hit Keep Warm/Cancel, and then hit Manual or Pressure Cook on High Pressure for 1 minute. When done, allow a 10-minute natural release followed by a quick release.

3 Transfer the quinoa to a large bowl and fluff with a fork.

JEFF'S TIP Chilling the peanuts with the salad can make them soggy instead of crunchy. To avoid this, top the salad with the peanuts *after* it chills in the fridge, just before serving.

4 Immediately add all the remaining ingredients, except for the peanuts, sesame seeds, and pepper flakes, and toss until fully combined.

5 Cover and refrigerate for 2 hours, then serve topped with the peanuts, sesame seeds, and crushed red pepper flakes (if using).

CILANTRO-LIME BASMATI RICE

Serves 6
PER SERVING
Calories: **273**
Fat: **4.7g**
Carbs: **52.3g**
Sodium: **12mg**
Protein: **4.9g**
Fiber: **1.8g**
Sugars: **0.8g**

 DF + *(if using avocado oil)*
GF
V

Fluffy basmati rice gets a simple but oh-so-rewarding twist here with just a bit of cilantro and lime. This super flavorful rice dish is low in sodium, pairs well with a wide range of cuisines, and is as easy as it gets.

Prep Time	Pressure Building Time	Pressure Cook Time	Natural Release Time	Total Time
5 MIN	5–10 MIN	5 MIN	10 MIN	25 MIN

2 cups basmati rice

2 cups water

Juice of 2 limes, divided, plus grated zest of 1 lime

1 tablespoon cumin seed (different from ground cumin)

½ cup chopped fresh cilantro

2 tablespoons ghee (store-bought or homemade, page 39) or avocado oil

1 teaspoon garlic salt

1 Put the rice in a fine-mesh strainer and rinse it under cold running water for 90 seconds, or until the water goes from cloudy to clear. Add the rice to the pot, along with the water, juice of 1 lime, and cumin seed. Stir well.

2 Secure the lid, move the valve to the sealing position, hit Keep Warm/Cancel, and then hit Manual or Pressure Cook on High Pressure for 5 minutes. When done, allow a 10-minute natural release followed by a quick release. Fluff the rice with a fork.

3 Add the juice and zest of the remaining lime, then the cilantro, ghee or avocado oil, and garlic salt. Stir until combined and serve.

 JEFF'S TIP If you can't find basmati rice, use any long-grain white rice. You can even substitute brown rice, but you'll need to increase the pressure cook time to 25 minutes (keep the 10-minute natural release). The nutrition facts are basically identical.

BRUSSELS SPROUT RISOTTO

Serves 6

PER SERVING
Calories: **214**
Fat: **9.1g**
Carbs: **25.5g**
Sodium: **303mg**
Protein: **8.2g**
Fiber: **5g**
Sugars: **3.7g**

Now hear me out. If the "little green balls of death" aren't your style, I was once like you. But I can promise that if you try them in this absolutely beautiful and lightened-up risotto, you'll see that Brussels sprouts can be rich and creamy, and will quickly become your best friends. Oh yeah, risotto is also one of the best reasons to own an Instant Pot. You'll see why.

Prep Time	Crisping Time	Sauté Time	Pressure Building Time	Pressure Cook Time	Total Time
5 MIN	10–15 MIN	5 MIN	10–15 MIN	6 MIN	35 MIN

1 pound Brussels sprouts, coarsely shredded or chopped (you can use a food processor)

2 tablespoons extra-virgin olive oil

Juice of 1 lemon

1 tablespoon ghee (store-bought or homemade, page 39)

2 shallots, diced

3 cloves garlic, minced or pressed

1/2 cup dry white wine (like a chardonnay) or additional broth

2 cups arborio rice (you must use this kind of rice to make a proper risotto)

4 1/2 cups Garlic Broth (page 44) or low-sodium vegetable broth

1 teaspoon seasoned salt

1/2 teaspoon black pepper

1/2 teaspoon Italian seasoning

1/2 cup grated Parmesan cheese

1 Put the Brussels sprouts in the Instant Pot, drizzle with the oil and lemon juice, and stir. Add the air fryer lid, hit Broil (400°F) for 10–15 minutes, and hit Start to begin. Broil until crispy. (NOTE: If you don't have an air fryer lid, place the sprouts on a foil-lined baking sheet, drizzle with the oil and lemon juice, and broil for 3–5 minutes, until crispy—but keep an eye on them so they don't burn, as ovens vary.)

2 Transfer the crisped Brussels sprouts to a bowl.

3 Add the ghee to the Instant Pot, hit Sauté, and Adjust so it's on the More or High setting. Once it's melted and bubbling, add the shallots and sauté for 2 minutes. Add the garlic and sauté for 1 minute. Add the wine and deglaze for 1 minute.

4 Add the rice, stir well, and cook for 1 minute, then add the broth and give everything another stir. Secure the lid, move the valve to the sealing position, hit Keep Warm/Cancel, and then hit Manual or Pressure Cook on High Pressure for 6 minutes. Quick release when done.

5 Add most of the crispy Brussels sprouts, the seasoned salt, pepper, Italian seasoning, and Parmesan. Stir until it's combined and creamy.

6 Serve topped with the remaining crispy Brussels sprouts.

JEFF'S TIP If Brussels sprouts aren't your thing, try this with half a head of cabbage instead—it's equally as delicious!

EGGPLANT RISOTTO

Serves 6

PER SERVING
Calories: **214**
Fat: **11.4g**
Carbs: **23.5g**
Sodium: **325mg**
Protein: **6.8g**
Fiber: **5.2g**
Sugars: **5.1g**

  DF + *(if using all olive oil)*

GF

V

Inspired by a trip to Israel, where eggplant is a culinary staple, I came up with this spectacular risotto, which tastes meaty without any meat whatsoever. Not only is it stunning on the eyes, it's also stunning on the taste buds.

Prep Time 5 MIN	**Sauté Time** 8 MIN	**Pressure Building Time** 10–15 MIN	**Pressure Cook Time** 6 MIN	**Total Time** 30 MIN

- 2 tablespoons extra-virgin olive oil
- 1 yellow onion, diced
- 1 medium carrot, peeled and diced
- 2 tablespoons ghee (store-bought or homemade, page 39) or additional olive oil
- 8 ounces baby bella mushrooms, sliced

- 2 cups arborio rice (you must use this kind of rice to make a proper risotto)
- 5 cups Garlic Broth (page 44) or low-sodium vegetable broth
- 1 large eggplant
- 1 teaspoon curry powder (optional)

- 1 teaspoon seasoned salt
- 1 teaspoon black pepper
- 1/2 teaspoon garlic salt
- 1/2 cup grated Parmesan cheese (optional)
- 1 tablespoon white or black truffle oil (optional)

1 Add the oil to the Instant Pot, hit Sauté, and Adjust so it's on the More or High setting.

2 After 3 minutes of heating, add the onion and carrot and sauté for 2 minutes. Add the ghee or additional oil and mushrooms and sauté for 2 minutes.

3 Add the rice, stir well, and cook for 1 minute, then add the broth and give everything another stir.

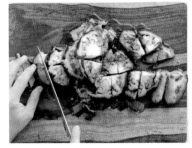

4 Top with the whole eggplant, or cut it in half if it's too big for the pot (see Jeff's Tip for a shortcut).

6 Remove the eggplant with tongs. Trim the stem end. Carefully quarter the eggplant lengthwise and then cut it crosswise into ½-inch slices. Return the eggplant to the pot and mix with the risotto.

5 Secure the lid, move the valve to the sealing position, hit Keep Warm/Cancel, and then hit Manual or Pressure Cook on High Pressure for 6 minutes. Quick release when done.

7 Season the risotto with the curry powder (if using), seasoned salt, pepper, garlic salt, grated Parmesan (if using), and truffle oil (if using). Stir well and serve.

JEFF'S TIP If you want to take a shortcut, instead of cutting up the whole eggplant after it pressure cooks and returning it to the pot in Step 6, you can cut it up raw and add it in Step 4, before pressure cooking. The difference is that cooking the eggplant whole makes for a meatier, heartier eggplant, whereas taking this shortcut will result in a slightly softer eggplant.

5

POULTRY

This chapter brings you uninterrupted Instant Pot gold.
I can say that with confidence because every bird
in here is wonderfully rich in flavor. And once you see how
easily it is done, you'll never be a chicken when it
comes to cooking it in an Instant Pot. Some recipes call for
lightly dredging (coating) the chicken in a simply
seasoned flour mixture and flash-searing it to give it a light
brown sear, additional flavor, and lovely texture. If that's
not for you, by all means, feel free to skip the step.

≈ = AIR FRYER LID   DF = DAIRY-FREE

K = KETO   GF = GLUTEN-FREE

P = PALEO   V = VEGETARIAN

+ = COMPLIANT WITH MODIFICATIONS   VN = VEGAN

CHICKEN CACCIATORE

Serves 6

PER SERVING
Calories: **333**
Fat: **17.3g**
Carbs: **16.2g**
Sodium: **244mg**
Protein: **41.3g**
Fiber: **3.8g**
Sugars: **9.5g**

Oh, Chicken Cacciatore, how I love you. The tomato sauce in this super hearty Italian stew is loaded with flavor and peppered with goodies from the pantry and the garden. I like to serve this over Cilantro-Lime Basmati Rice (page 130).

Prep Time	Sauté Time	Pressure Building Time	Pressure Cook Time	Total Time
5 MIN	15 MIN	10–15 MIN	6 MIN	40 MIN

- 3 tablespoons extra-virgin olive oil
- 1 tablespoon ghee (store-bought or homemade, page 39; optional)
- 3 pounds bone-in, skinless chicken thighs and drumsticks (I pulled the skin off the drumsticks), seasoned with a little salt and pepper
- 1 Vidalia (sweet) onion, diced
- 2 green bell peppers, seeded and diced

- 8 ounces baby bella mushrooms, sliced
- 6 cloves garlic, minced or pressed
- ¼ cup dry red wine (like a pinot noir) or additional broth
- 1 cup canned no-salt-added crushed tomatoes
- 1 (14.5-ounce) can no-salt-added diced tomatoes, with their juices
- ¼ cup low-sodium chicken broth
- 1 teaspoon seasoned salt

- 1 teaspoon black pepper
- 1 teaspoon dried sage
- 1 teaspoon dried thyme
- 1 (6-ounce) can no-salt-added tomato paste
- 2 tablespoons red wine vinegar
- 1 teaspoon raw honey (optional)
- ¼ cup Spanish olives, pitted and sliced (optional)
- ¼ cup kalamata olives, pitted and sliced (optional)

1 Add the oil and ghee (if using) to the Instant Pot, hit Sauté, and Adjust so it's on the More or High setting. Once the oil's bubbling and the ghee's melted (about 3 minutes), add the chicken in batches and flash-sear for 20 seconds on each side. Using tongs, transfer the chicken to a plate and set aside.

2 Add the onion, peppers, and mushrooms to the pot and sauté, stirring occasionally, for about 5 minutes, until slightly softened. Add the garlic and sauté for 1 minute.

CONTINUES

3 Add the wine to deglaze the bottom of the pot and let simmer for 1 minute. Really make sure the bottom of the pot is as smooth as possible with any browned bits scraped up from the deglazing.

4 Add the crushed tomatoes, diced tomatoes, broth, seasoned salt, pepper, sage, and thyme. Stir until well combined, then return the chicken to the pot.

5 Secure the lid, move the valve to the sealing position, hit Keep Warm/Cancel, and then hit Manual or Pressure Cook on High Pressure for 6 minutes. Quick release when done. Using tongs, transfer the chicken to a serving dish.

6 Add the tomato paste, vinegar, honey (if using), and olives (if using) to the pot. Stir until well combined. Let sit for 5 minutes for the sauce to thicken.

7 Pour the sauce over the chicken and serve.

 JEFF'S TIP If olives aren't your salty style, add some roasted red peppers instead.

HERBACEOUS ROASTED CHICKEN

Serves 6

PER SERVING
Calories: **308**
Fat: **25.2g**
Carbs: **5.2g**
Sodium: **136mg**
Protein: **17.6g**
Fiber: **0.9g**
Sugars: **1.2g**

K + *(if you don't mind a slurry)*

P + *(if you don't mind a slurry)*

GF

This one brings a whole new meaning to "chicken in a pot." As easy as it is delicious, this recipe results in one of the juiciest chickens you'll ever sink your teeth into. Whether or not you choose the optional final step of giving it a gorgeous, golden crisp, this chicken will make your mouth water. The chicken goes wonderfully with Brussels Sprout Risotto (page 132) or Cauliflower Aligot (page 236).

Prep Time	Pressure Building Time	Pressure Cook Time	Natural Release Time	Optional Crisping Time	Sauté Time	Total Time
10 MIN	10–15 MIN	30 MIN	10 MIN	5–10 MIN	2 MIN	1 HR 15 MIN

THE CHICKEN

3 tablespoons ghee (store-bought or homemade, page 39)

3 tablespoons extra-virgin olive oil

1/2 teaspoon paprika

1/2 teaspoon dried thyme

1/2 teaspoon dried sage

1/2 teaspoon lemon pepper seasoning

1/2 teaspoon seasoned salt

3 cloves garlic, minced or pressed

1 (5-pound) whole chicken, giblets removed from cavity and discarded

3/4 cup low-sodium chicken broth or Garlic Broth (page 44)

1 large carrot, peeled and diced

2 ribs celery, cut into 1/4-inch pieces

THE GRAVY

2 tablespoons cornstarch or arrowroot powder

2 tablespoons cold water

1 tablespoon unsweetened nondairy milk

2 teaspoons lemon pepper seasoning

1 teaspoon dried sage

— THE CHICKEN —

1 Put the ghee in a microwave-safe bowl and microwave for 25 seconds, or until melted. Add the oil, paprika, thyme, sage, lemon pepper, seasoned salt, and garlic and stir until combined. Pour one-third of the mixture into a small bowl and reserve to season the chicken after it's cooked.

CONTINUES

2 Place the trivet on a cutting board and place the chicken on it, breast side down (this makes it easy to transfer to the Instant Pot). Brush the back of the chicken with the ghee marinade, then flip it over and brush the breast side. (NOTE: To infuse the chicken with even more flavor, you can cut small slits in the skin, without cutting through the meat, to allow the marinade to seep in.)

3 Add the broth, carrot, and celery to the Instant Pot. Lower the trivet with the basted chicken on it (still breast side up) into the pot, secure the lid, move the valve to the sealing position, and hit Manual or Pressure Cook on High Pressure for 6 minutes per pound of chicken. (I used a 5-pound chicken, so that's 30 minutes. If you used a 4½-pound chicken, that would be 27 minutes, and so on.) When done, allow a 10-minute natural release followed by a quick release.

4 Once the lid comes off the pot, don't worry if some of the chicken begins to come a little loose and the wings are barely holding on. This is normal because of how tender it will be.

5 If the reserved marinade has solidified by now, just put it in the microwave for 10 seconds and stir. With a clean brush, dab (don't brush) the breast of the chicken with the marinade. (If you brush, it will knock all those lovely seasonings off the chicken.)

CONTINUES

JEFF'S TIPS

If you don't serve the gravy, you can shave off about 6g fat. If you don't eat the skin, that'll shave off about another 6g fat.

When the chicken cooks, the breast cavity (where the wishbone is) may tend to want to split. This is because it's so tender! Should you wish it to remain intact, simply tie the ends of the legs together with kitchen twine prior to pressure cooking.

6 Should you wish to give your chicken a nice crisp and beautiful color (highly recommended), add the air fryer lid, hit Broil (400°F) for 5–10 minutes (I went for 10 minutes), and hit Start to begin. Alternatively, you can transfer the chicken to a foil-lined baking sheet and broil it in the oven for 3–5 minutes (keep an eye on it, as ovens vary). Just be careful not to go for too long so you don't dry it out.

7 Carefully transfer the chicken to a serving platter. Now let's make some gravy with all those glorious drippings in the pot!

THE GRAVY

8 Mix together the cornstarch and water to form a slurry.

9 Hit Keep Warm/Cancel, hit Sauté, and Adjust so it's on the More or High setting. Once the juices in the pot bubble, immediately stir in the slurry. Allow it to bubble for about 30 seconds, then hit Keep Warm/Cancel to turn off the pot. Stir in the milk, lemon pepper seasoning, and sage. Stir until combined and you will have the perfect gravy.

10 Transfer the gravy to a gravy boat and serve with the chicken as desired.

JEFFREY'S FAVORITE CHICKEN

Serves 6

PER SERVING
Calories: **372**
Fat: **17g**
Carbs: **13.1g**
Sodium: **520mg**
Protein: **36.8g**
Fiber: **3g**
Sugars: **3.5g**

K + *(if you dredge with coconut flour and don't mind a slurry)*

P + *(if you dredge with coconut flour and don't mind a slurry)*

GF + *(if you dredge with coconut or quinoa flour)*

This is one of the most glorious recipes in this book, loaded with mushrooms, sun-dried tomatoes, and artichokes, whose flavors linger on the tongue so pleasantly. In fact, the sauce is so good you'll want to drink it—and seeing as wine is a key ingredient, you just might.

Prep Time	Sauté Time	Pressure Building Time	Pressure Cook Time	Total Time
10 MIN	15 MIN	10–15 MIN	5 MIN	40 MIN

- **2 pounds boneless, skinless chicken breasts, sliced horizontally into ¼-inch-thick cutlets**
- **¼ cup whole-wheat flour, coconut flour, or quinoa flour (with a few pinches of garlic powder, black pepper, and kosher salt mixed in)**
- **¼ cup extra-virgin olive oil**
- **2 teaspoons ghee (store-bought or homemade, page 39), divided**
- **2 large shallots, diced**

- **8 ounces baby bella mushrooms, sliced**
- **6 cloves garlic, minced or pressed**
- **½ cup dry white wine (like a sauvignon blanc) or additional broth**
- **Juice of ½ lemon**
- **½ cup low-sodium chicken broth**
- **1 teaspoon Italian seasoning**
- **1 teaspoon seasoned salt**

- **5–8 ounces baby spinach**
- **1 tablespoon cornstarch or arrowroot powder**
- **1 tablespoon cold water**
- **¼ cup unsweetened nondairy milk**
- **1 (10-ounce) jar sun-dried tomatoes, drained and roughly chopped**
- **1 (14-ounce) can artichoke hearts, drained and chopped**

1 Dredge the chicken cutlets in the flour mixture so they're lightly coated and set aside on a plate. (It's okay if some of the mixture is left over.)

2 Add the oil and 1 teaspoon of the ghee to the Instant Pot, hit Sauté, and Adjust to the More or High setting. Once the oil's bubbling and the ghee's melted (about 3 minutes), add the chicken in batches and lightly brown for 45 seconds on each side. Use tongs to transfer to a plate.

3 Add the remaining 1 teaspoon of ghee to the pot. Once it's melted and bubbling, add the shallots and mushrooms and sauté for 2 minutes. Add the garlic and sauté for 1 minute.

CONTINUES

4 Add the wine and lemon juice and simmer for 2 minutes, scraping the bottom of the pot to loosen any browned bits.

5 Add the broth, Italian seasoning, and seasoned salt and stir. Return the chicken to the pot and top with the spinach (don't worry if it seems piled a bit high—it cooks down into nothing).

6 Secure the lid, move the valve to the sealing position, hit Keep Warm/Cancel, and then hit Manual or Pressure Cook on High Pressure for 5 minutes. Quick release when done.

7 Use tongs to transfer the chicken to a serving dish.

8 Mix together the cornstarch and water to form a slurry.

9 Hit Keep Warm/Cancel, Sauté, and Adjust so it's on the More or High setting. Once bubbling, stir in the slurry and let bubble for 30 seconds, then hit Keep Warm/Cancel again to turn off the pot. Stir in the milk, sun-dried tomatoes, and artichokes. Let rest for 5 minutes to thicken a bit.

10 Ladle the sauce over the chicken and serve.

JEFF'S TIP The only tip I have for this recipe is that you need to make it and then tell me about it.

LEMON ORZO CHICKEN

Serves 6

PER SERVING
Calories: **315**
Fat: **15.5g**
Carbs: **6.7g**
Sodium: **331mg**
Protein: **36.7g**
Fiber: **1.4g**
Sugars: **1.8g**

I was annoyed that I devised this recipe just *after* I finished writing my first cookbook, and didn't get to include it. I vowed then that should I write another cookbook, this one would be in it. Similar to a Greek avgolemono soup, this dish features a lemony egg sauce touched with a hint of orzo to adorn the chicken. Serve with my Acorn Squash Mash (page 226).

Prep Time	Sauté Time	Pressure Building Time	Pressure Cook Time	Total Time
10 MIN	10 MIN	10–15 MIN	6 MIN	40 MIN

- **2 pounds boneless, skinless chicken breasts, sliced horizontally into ¼-inch-thick cutlets (many markets sell them already sliced thin)**
- **¼ cup whole-wheat flour, coconut flour, or quinoa flour (with a few pinches of garlic powder, black pepper, and kosher salt mixed in)**

- **¼ cup extra-virgin olive oil**
- **2 teaspoons ghee (store-bought or homemade, page 39), divided**
- **2 large shallots, diced**
- **1¾ cups low-sodium chicken broth**
- **⅓ cup whole-wheat orzo (see Jeff's Tip)**

- **5 ounces baby spinach (optional)**
- **1 large egg**
- **Juice of 2 lemons**
- **¼ cup grated Parmesan cheese (optional)**

1 Dredge the chicken cutlets in the flour mixture so they're lightly coated and set aside on a plate. (It's okay if some of the mixture is left over.)

2 Add the oil and 1 teaspoon of the ghee to the Instant Pot, hit Sauté, and Adjust to the More or High setting. Once the oil's bubbling and the ghee's melted (about 3 minutes), add the chicken in batches and lightly brown, about 45 seconds on each side. Use tongs to transfer to a plate.

3 Add the remaining 1 teaspoon of ghee to the pot. Once it's melted and bubbling, add the shallots and sauté for 2 minutes. Scrape the bottom of the pot to loosen any flour that may have been caked on from browning the chicken.

4 Add the broth and orzo to the pot, then add the chicken. Smooth the orzo out so it's submerged in the broth and around the chicken. Top with the spinach (if using) but *do not stir;* just let it rest on top of everything else.

5 Secure the lid, move the valve to the sealing position, hit Keep Warm/Cancel, and then hit Manual or Pressure Cook on High Pressure for 6 minutes. Quick release when done.

6 Using tongs, transfer the chicken to a serving dish (it's fine if a lot of the spinach gets transferred with the chicken, but leave the liquid and orzo in the pot).

7 In a measuring cup or small bowl, whisk together the egg and lemon juice. Pour the mixture into the sauce in the pot while stirring. You'll see it thicken up perfectly, with a few egg ribbons forming. Stir in the Parmesan, if using.

8 Spoon the sauce over the chicken and serve.

JEFF'S TIP Want this dish to be a bit less carby? Sub cauliflower rice for the orzo, but add it in Step 7 so it doesn't dissolve under pressure. You'll save only about 2g of carbs, though, so I say go for the orzo—there's not much of it and it's not the star of the dish, just a delightful accent.

CAROLINA PULLED CHICKEN WITH SLAW

Meet pulled pork's sassier yet leaner cousin. This one is perfect any time of year, but it works especially well in the warmer months when you can dine in the yard (or on the terrace). Although commonly eaten in a sandwich, the sweet, sour, and savory pulled chicken is equally delicious when tossed with a salad. The optional slaw gives it a cool, crisp touch.

Serves 6

PER SERVING
with/without slaw

Calories: **305/268**

Fat: **4.3g/3.8g**

Carbs: **22.3g/21.8g**

Sodium: **591mg/536mg**

Protein: **35.4g/32.6g**

Fiber: **1.6g/0g**

Sugars: **11.7g/8.2g**

 + *(if using sugar-free steak sauce and no slaw)*

 DF

GF

Prep Time	Sauté Time	Pressure Building Time	Pressure Cook Time	Total Time
10 MIN	**1** MINUTE	**10–15** MIN	**12** MIN	**35** MIN

THE SLAW (OPTIONAL)

1 (12-ounce) bag shredded coleslaw mix

½ cup plain 2% Greek yogurt (store-bought or homemade, page 36) or low-fat mayonnaise

1 tablespoon pure maple syrup

2 teaspoons fresh lemon juice

1½ teaspoons white vinegar

1 teaspoon paprika

1 teaspoon black pepper

½ teaspoon seasoned salt

THE CHICKEN

1 cup low-sodium chicken broth

2 pounds boneless, skinless chicken breasts

THE CAROLINA SAUCE

¼ cup pure maple syrup

¼ cup raw honey

¼ cup Dijon mustard

2 tablespoons Worcestershire sauce or sugar-free steak sauce

2 tablespoons apple cider vinegar

2 tablespoons hot sauce (optional)

1 teaspoon liquid smoke (I use hickory flavor)

1 teaspoon onion powder

1 teaspoon garlic powder

1 If you're making the slaw, combine all the slaw ingredients in a large bowl and toss well to mix. Cover and refrigerate until ready to serve.

2 To make the chicken, put the broth and chicken in the pot. Secure the lid, move the valve to the sealing position, hit Keep Warm/Cancel, and then hit Manual or Pressure Cook on High Pressure for 12 minutes (or up to 17 if using very thick breasts). Quick release when done.

3 While the chicken's cooking or releasing, whisk together the Carolina sauce ingredients in a bowl.

4 Transfer the chicken to a bowl (you can discard the liquid or save it for a rainy day). Shred the chicken with two forks or an electric mixer (this makes life so easy!). Add the Carolina sauce and toss until combined. Serve with the slaw, if desired.

JEFF'S TIP Feel free to serve up this dish any way you like it. Wrapping the pulled chicken and slaw in romaine or Bibb lettuce leaves is wonderful!

CREAMY AVOCADO CHICKEN

Serves 6

PER SERVING
Calories: **434**
Fat: **20.1g**
Carbs: **10.7g**
Sodium: **304mg**
Protein: **52.4g**
Fiber: **5.1g**
Sugars: **2.3g**

I'm obsessed with guacamole. So much, in fact, that I wanted to turn it into a sauce—especially since avocado is one of the healthiest fats out there. Once we stir this flowing, spectacular sauce into tender chicken, the result is lush and wonderful. Serve on a bed of my Quintessential Quinoa (page 116).

Prep Time	Sauté Time	Pressure Building Time	Pressure Cook Time	Total Time
10 MIN	10 MIN	5–10 MIN	4 MIN	30 MIN

THE CHICKEN

- 2 tablespoons avocado oil or extra-virgin olive oil
- 1 red onion, diced
- 3 cloves garlic, minced or pressed
- 3 pounds boneless, skinless chicken breasts, cut into bite-size pieces
- 1 cup low-sodium chicken broth

THE AVOCADO PUREE

- 2 ripe avocados, peeled, pitted, and halved, divided
- 1 large shallot, diced
- 2 tablespoons chopped fresh cilantro, plus more for garnish (optional)
- 1 jalapeño pepper, seeded and diced (optional)
- ½ cup plain 2% Greek yogurt (store-bought or homemade, page 36)
- 2 tablespoons avocado oil or extra-virgin olive oil
- Juice of 1 lime
- 1 teaspoon hot sauce, plus more for garnish (optional)
- 1 teaspoon seasoned salt
- 1 teaspoon garlic powder
- 1 teaspoon dried oregano

1 To make the chicken, add the oil to the Instant Pot, hit Sauté, and Adjust to the More or High setting. Once the oil's bubbling and the ghee's melted (about 3 minutes), add the onion and sauté for 3 minutes, or until lightly softened. Add the garlic and sauté for 1 minute.

2 Add the chicken and sauté for about 3 minutes, until it turns pinkish-white.

3 Add the broth to the pot and smooth out the chicken so it's submerged. Secure the lid, move the valve to the sealing position, hit Keep Warm/Cancel, and then hit Manual or Pressure Cook on High Pressure for 4 minutes. Quick release when done.

4 Meanwhile, combine 3 of the avocado halves and all of the remaining avocado puree ingredients in a food processor or blender and puree until smooth. It will be very thick, like guacamole (and feel free to enjoy it on its own as such).

5 When the Instant Pot lid comes off, it will look very liquidy. (See Jeff's Tip if you'd like a thick final sauce.) Add the avocado puree to the pot and stir until it's fully melded into the broth. From there, it will thicken into a wonderful sauce.

6 Slice the remaining avocado half into thin slivers. Serve the chicken and avocado sauce topped with additional cilantro (if using), a few shakes of hot sauce (if using), and a few slivers of avocado.

JEFF'S TIP If you'd like to guarantee a thicker final sauce, you'll want to remove some broth in Step 5 before adding the avocado. I strongly suggest you ladle out half to three-quarters of the broth, then add the avocado puree to the pot. After adding the puree, if you decide you want the sauce thinner, stir some broth back in until it's the desired consistency. Remember, you can always make it thinner after you add the puree, but you can't make it thicker. So if you leave all the broth in before adding the puree, you'll have a very runny, thin sauce (which I don't recommend).

CHICKEN WITH CHINESE BLACK BEAN SAUCE

Serves 6

PER SERVING
Calories: **310**
Fat: **11g**
Carbs: **13g**
Sodium: **525mg**
Protein: **34.9g**
Fiber: **2.6g**
Sugars: **5g**

One of my all-time favorite dishes in Chinese American cuisine, chicken in black bean sauce, is made with soybeans that are fermented, giving them a delightful, savory flavor that produces an unforgettable sauce. If you've not tried this before and are a fan of the savory experience, prepare to sign up.

Prep Time	Sauté Time	Pressure Building Time	Pressure Cook Time	Total Time
10 MIN	15 MIN	5–10 MIN	4 MIN	35 MIN

3 tablespoons sesame oil

1 large yellow onion, sliced into thick wedges

1 large red bell pepper, seeded and diced

15 green beans, ends trimmed

25 snow peapods

1 bunch scallions, sliced

6 cloves garlic, sliced into thin slivers

2 pounds boneless, skinless chicken breasts, sliced horizontally into ¼-inch-thick cutlets and then cut crosswise into ¼-inch-thick strips

1 tablespoon minced or grated ginger

2 tablespoons Shaoxing wine or dry sherry

2 teaspoons coconut aminos, low-sodium soy sauce, or tamari

1 cup low-sodium chicken broth

1 tablespoon cornstarch or arrowroot powder

1 tablespoon cold water

⅓ cup fermented black beans (see Jeff's Tip), plus more for optional garnish

Sliced scallions, for topping

1 Add the oil to the Instant Pot, hit Sauté, and Adjust so it's on the More or High setting. After 3 minutes of heating, add the onion, bell pepper, green beans, peapods, scallions (reserve a few for garnish), and garlic. Sauté, stirring occasionally, for about 5 minutes, until the veggies are slightly softened.

2 Add the chicken and sauté for about 2 minutes, until it turns pinkish-white.

3 Add the ginger, wine, and coconut aminos. Let simmer for 1 minute, then add the broth.

4 Secure the lid, move the valve to the sealing position, hit Keep Warm/Cancel, and then hit Manual or Pressure Cook on High Pressure for 4 minutes. Quick release when done.

5 Mix together the cornstarch and water to form a slurry.

6 Hit Keep Warm/Cancel, hit Sauté, and Adjust so it's on the More or High setting. Once bubbling, stir in the slurry and black beans and let bubble for 30 seconds, then hit Keep Warm/Cancel again to turn off the pot. Let rest for 5 minutes to slightly thicken.

7 Serve topped with scallions and additional fermented black beans, if desired.

JEFF'S TIP Fermented black beans, aka douchi, can be found in most Asian markets and online. You can also use ¼ cup of low-sodium black bean sauce, which can be found in the Asian or international aisle of many supermarkets. Bear in mind that fermented black beans are not interchangeable with typical black beans as they're soybeans.

DIJON DILL CHICKEN

This is a chicken dish with a sauce so good, I tend to put it on everything (check out my first cookbook for a pork tenderloin variation). The combination of Dijon, dill, and lemon is beyond delicious as it cascades over the melt-in-your-mouth chicken. The whole thing goes extraordinarily well with my Carrot & Shallot "Fried" Rice (page 118), which will sop up that luscious sauce so beautifully!

Serves 6

PER SERVING
Calories: **320**
Fat: **11.1g**
Carbs: **6.1g**
Sodium: **768mg**
Protein: **41.2g**
Fiber: **0.3g**
Sugars: **0.6g**

 K + *(if you don't mind a slurry)*

P + *(if you don't mind a slurry)*

GF

Prep Time	Pressure Building Time	Pressure Cook Time	Sauté Time	Total Time
5 MIN	5–10 MIN	6 MIN	2 MIN	20 MIN

1½ cups low-sodium chicken broth

½ cup Dijon mustard, divided

3 pounds boneless, skinless chicken thighs or 2 pounds boneless, skinless chicken breasts (If you use thighs, keep them whole. If you use breasts, cut into bite-size pieces.)

3 tablespoons ghee (store-bought or homemade, page 39)

1 teaspoon seasoned salt

Juice of ½ lemon

2 tablespoons cornstarch or arrowroot powder

2 tablespoons cold water

½ cup chopped or torn fresh dill, plus more for garnish

1 Combine the broth and ¼ cup of the Dijon mustard in the Instant Pot and stir to mix. Add the chicken and top off with the ghee. (NOTE: If you want the sauce to have an even stronger dill flavor, add the dill now rather than waiting until Step 7.)

3 Use tongs to transfer the chicken to a serving bowl.

2 Secure the lid, move the valve to the sealing position, and hit Manual or Pressure Cook on High Pressure for 6 minutes. Quick release when done.

4 Hit Keep Warm/Cancel, Sauté, and Adjust so it's on the More or High setting. Add the seasoned salt, lemon juice, and remaining ¼ cup of Dijon mustard. Stir until combined.

5 Mix together the cornstarch and water to form a slurry.

6 Once the pot is bubbling, add the slurry and stir for 30 seconds, then hit Keep Warm/Cancel again to turn off the pot. As the bubbles die down, the sauce will have thickened significantly. Let it cool for about 5 minutes.

7 Stir in the dill, then pour the sauce over the chicken. (NOTE: If you already added the dill in Step 1 and still want more, simply stir however much more you'd like into the sauce now.)

8 Serve topped with additional fresh dill, if desired.

JEFF'S TIP Want it more lemony? Add the juice of a whole lemon instead of just half.

CHIMICHURRI CHICKEN

Serves 6

PER SERVING
Calories: **440**
Fat: **25g**
Carbs: **3.5g**
Sodium: **143mg**
Protein: **48.8g**
Fiber: **0.6g**
Sugars: **0.7g**

Chimichurri is an Argentinean herb sauce that adds fresh, bright, and mildly spicy notes to anything it is paired with. It focuses on parsley as the main ingredient, which is then blended with olive oil, garlic, vinegar, and a few basic spices. When married with chicken, it becomes a wedding you definitely want an invitation to. Enjoy with my Crispy Kale Rice (page 124).

Prep Time	Sauté Time	Pressure Building Time	Pressure Cook Time	Total Time
5 MIN	**10** MIN	**5–10** MIN	**4** MIN	**25** MIN

THE CHICKEN

2 tablespoons avocado oil or extra-virgin olive oil

2 large shallots, roughly chopped

2 pounds boneless, skinless chicken breasts and/or thighs, cut into bite-size pieces

1/2 cup low-sodium chicken broth

THE CHIMICHURRI SAUCE

1 cup packed fresh flat-leaf parsley

4 cloves garlic, peeled

1/2 cup extra-virgin olive oil

1 tablespoon red wine vinegar

1 tablespoon balsamic vinegar

1 teaspoon seasoned salt

1/2 teaspoon onion powder

1/2 teaspoon garlic powder

1/2 teaspoon dried oregano

1/2 teaspoon ground cumin

1/2 teaspoon chili powder (optional)

1 Add the oil to the Instant Pot, hit Sauté, and Adjust to the More or High setting. After 3 minutes of heating, add the shallots and sauté for 3 minutes, until lightly softened.

2 Add the chicken and sauté for about 3 minutes, until it turns pinkish-white.

3 Add the broth. Secure the lid, move the valve to the sealing position, hit Keep Warm/Cancel, and then hit Manual or Pressure Cook on High Pressure for 4 minutes. Quick release when done.

4 Meanwhile, while the chicken cooks, in a food processor or blender, combine all the chimichurri ingredients and puree until smooth.

5 Using a slotted spoon, transfer the chicken and shallots to a serving dish (it's okay if some of the broth makes it in, but not too much).

6 Pour the chimichurri over the chicken, mix until fully coated, and serve.

JEFF'S TIP Either avocado oil or extra-virgin olive oil will work beautifully in the chimichurri sauce. Feel free to add a mix of both!

LEMON PEPPER WINGS

Serves 8

PER SERVING
Calories: **578**
Fat: **42.7g**
Carbs: **0.1g**
Sodium: **144mg**
Protein: **45.8g**
Fiber: **0g**
Sugars: **0g**

Wings are one of the many things that the Instant Pot does right. Here, we have a simple, two-step process in which we pressure cook them to juicy perfection and then finish them up with a lemon pepper glaze that crisps up after a few minutes of broiling, either with the air fryer lid or in the oven.

Prep Time	Pressure Building Time	Pressure Cook Time	Optional Crisping Time	Total Time
5 MIN	5-10 MIN	8 MIN	10-15 MIN	30 MIN

THE WINGS

Lemon pepper seasoning

3 pounds chicken wings, separated at the joint (in many markets you can easily find them already separated)

THE LEMON PEPPER GLAZE

6 tablespoons ghee (store-bought or homemade, page 39), melted

1½ teaspoons lemon pepper seasoning

½ teaspoon garlic powder

½ teaspoon dried parsley

1 Lightly rub the lemon-pepper seasoning all over the chicken wings.

2 Place the trivet in the Instant Pot, pour in 1 cup of water, and place the wings on top (you can also place the wings in a steamer basket instead of resting them on the trivet, as I did). Secure the lid, move the valve to the sealing position, and hit Manual or Pressure Cook on High Pressure for 8 minutes. Quick release when done.

3 While the wings are pressure cooking, stir together the lemon pepper glaze ingredients in a bowl until combined.

4 Transfer the wings to a bowl and drain the water from the pot.

5 If you want to crisp up the wings (highly recommended!), add the air fryer basket or trivet to the pot, coat with nonstick spray, and place as many wings as you can in it. Brush the lemon pepper glaze onto the wings. (If you don't want to crisp the wings, just brush on the glaze now and you're done.)

6 Add the air fryer lid, hit Broil (400°F) for 10–15 minutes, and hit Start to begin. Midway through the crisping process, flip the wings and glaze the other side (the longer you go, the crispier the wings get, so be sure to check on them).

7 Transfer the wings to a serving bowl and slather on any remaining glaze before serving!

JEFF'S TIPS To crisp the wings in an oven, line a baking sheet with aluminum foil and coat with nonstick spray. Place the wings on the sheet and broil for 5–10 minutes, until fully crisped, flipping over midway through to glaze the other side. (In order to reach the desired crispiness, keep an eye on it, as ovens vary.)

While the crisping is optional, I feel like it makes a world of difference.

EPIC BALSAMIC CHICKEN

Serves 6

PER SERVING
Calories: **338**
Fat: **17g**
Carbs: **9.3g**
Sodium: **161mg**
Protein: **34.5g**
Fiber: **0.9g**
Sugars: **3.8g**

 (if you dredge with coconut or quinoa flour)

This dish is basically the pot roast of the chicken world. Here, I take a classic balsamic chicken but dress it to the nines with a slew of rich vegetables to make it a complete meal in and of itself!

Prep Time	Sauté Time	Pressure Building Time	Pressure Cook Time	Total Time
10 MIN	15 MIN	10–15 MIN	10 MIN	50 MIN

- **2 pounds boneless, skinless chicken breasts, sliced horizontally into ¼-inch-thick cutlets**
- **¼ cup whole-wheat flour, coconut flour, or quinoa flour (with a few pinches of garlic powder, black pepper, and kosher salt mixed in)**
- **¼ cup extra-virgin olive oil**

- **2 tablespoons ghee (store-bought or homemade, page 39), divided**
- **1 yellow onion, cut into thick wedges**
- **⅓ cup balsamic vinegar**
- **¾ cup low-sodium chicken broth**
- **½ pound baby red or gold potatoes, halved**

- **1 large carrot, peeled and sliced into ¼-inch disks**
- **8 ounces portobello mushroom caps, sliced**
- **12 stalks asparagus, tough bottoms snapped or cut off**
- **1 tablespoon cornstarch or arrowroot powder**
- **1 tablespoon cold water**

1 Dredge the chicken cutlets in the flour mixture so they're lightly coated and set aside on a plate. (It's okay if some of the mixture is left over.)

2 Add the oil and 1 tablespoon of the ghee to the Instant Pot, hit Sauté, and Adjust to the More or High setting. Once the oil's bubbling and the ghee's melted (about 3 minutes), add the chicken in batches and lightly brown for about 45 seconds on each side. Use tongs to transfer to a plate.

3 Add the remaining 1 tablespoon of ghee to the pot. Once it's melted and bubbling, add the onion and sauté for 2 minutes. Add the balsamic vinegar and deglaze the bottom of the pot.

CONTINUES

4 Add the broth to the pot and lay in the trivet. Return the lightly browned chicken to the pot and rest on the trivet.

5 In the following order, layer the potatoes, mushrooms, carrot, and asparagus. (NOTE: It's important to follow this layering order because the veggies that cook most quickly should be farthest from the bottom of the pot.)

6 Secure the lid, move the valve to the sealing position, hit Keep Warm/Cancel, and then hit Manual or Pressure Cook on High Pressure for 10 minutes. Quick release when done.

7 Carefully lift out the trivet with the veggies and put them in a serving dish. Then, use tongs to transfer the chicken to the same dish.

8 Mix together the cornstarch and water to form a slurry.

9 Hit Keep Warm/Cancel, hit Sauté, and Adjust so it's on the More or High setting. Once bubbling, stir in the slurry and let bubble for 30 seconds, then hit Keep Warm/Cancel again to turn off the pot. Let rest 5 minutes to thicken a bit. Ladle the sauce over the chicken and veggies and serve.

JEFF'S TIP To give this dish an extra fancy final touch, feel free to drizzle a little balsamic glaze over each portion. You can find balsamic glaze in small bottles next to the vinegars, oils, and salad dressings in most markets.

BUBBE'S JEWISH CHICKEN POT

Of course I had to have a Jewish dish in this book. *Bubbe* (pronounced "bub-bee") is Yiddish for "Grandma." Growing up in a Jewish American household, I was introduced to the most wonderful chicken dishes loaded with fragrant veggies that made everyone run into the kitchen to see what was cooking in the pot. What was it? Bubbe's Jewish Chicken Pot. This goes nicely with brown rice (page 114).

Serves 6

PER SERVING
Calories: **396**
Fat: **15g**
Carbs: **10.5g**
Sodium: **400mg**
Protein: **50.6g**
Fiber: **2g**
Sugars: **2.5g**

 (if you dredge with coconut flour and don't mind a slurry)

 (if you dredge with coconut flour and don't mind a slurry)

 DF

GF *(if you dredge with coconut or quinoa flour)*

Prep Time	Sauté Time	Pressure Building Time	Pressure Cook Time	Total Time
5 MIN	15 MIN	10–15 MIN	6 MIN	40 MIN

- 3 pounds boneless, skinless chicken thighs or breasts (If you use thighs, keep them whole. If you use breasts, cut into bite-size pieces.)
- ¼ cup whole-wheat flour, coconut flour, or quinoa flour (with a few pinches of garlic powder, black pepper, and kosher salt mixed in)
- ¼ cup extra-virgin olive oil
- 2 teaspoons ghee (store-bought or homemade, page 39), divided (optional)

- 1 large yellow onion, diced
- 1 large carrot, peeled and diced
- 2 ribs celery, diced, with leafy tops reserved
- 13 cloves garlic, 10 halved and 3 minced or pressed
- ¼ cup dry white wine (like a chardonnay) or additional broth
- 1 cup low-sodium chicken broth
- ¼ cup chopped fresh parsley, plus more for garnish

- 1 teaspoon paprika
- ½ teaspoon poultry seasoning
- ½ teaspoon herbes de Provence or Italian seasoning
- ½ teaspoon dried thyme
- ½ teaspoon dried sage
- 1 teaspoon seasoned salt, divided
- ½ teaspoon black pepper
- 1 tablespoon cornstarch or arrowroot powder
- 1 tablespoon cold water

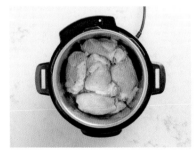

1 Dredge the chicken in the flour mixture so it's lightly coated and set aside on a plate. (It's okay if some of the mixture is left over.)

2 Add the oil and 1 teaspoon of the ghee (if using) to the Instant Pot, hit Sauté, and Adjust to the More or High setting. Once the oil's bubbling and the ghee's melted (about 3 minutes), add the chicken in batches and lightly brown for about 30 seconds on each side. Use tongs to transfer the chicken to a plate. (It's okay if there are still some browned bits of chicken stuck to the bottom of the pot.)

CONTINUES

3 Add the remaining 1 teaspoon of ghee (if using) to the pot. Once it's melted and bubbling, scrape up any chicken remnants and add the onion, carrot, diced celery, and halved garlic cloves and sauté for 6 minutes. Add the minced garlic and sauté for 1 minute.

4 Add the wine and simmer for 1 minute, scraping the bottom of the pot to loosen any browned bits.

5 Add the broth, parsley, paprika, poultry seasoning, herbes de Provence, thyme, sage, ½ teaspoon of the seasoned salt, and pepper. Stir well. Return the chicken to the pot.

6 Secure the lid, move the valve to the sealing position, hit Keep Warm/Cancel, and then hit Manual or Pressure Cook on High Pressure for 6 minutes. Quick release when done.

7 Using tongs, transfer the chicken to a serving dish. Add the reserved leafy tops from the celery and remaining ½ teaspoon of seasoned salt to the pot.

8 Mix together the cornstarch and water to form a slurry.

9 Hit Keep Warm/Cancel, Sauté, and Adjust so it's on the More or High setting. Once bubbling, stir in the slurry and let bubble for 30 seconds, then hit Keep Warm/Cancel again to turn off the pot.

10 Ladle the sauce over the chicken and serve with additional fresh parsley.

JEFF'S TIP

For a slightly creamy finish, add ¼ cup unsweetened nondairy milk after adding the slurry in Step 9.

CHICKEN FRA DIAVOLO

Serves 6

PER SERVING
Calories: **460**
Fat: **14.9g**
Carbs: **8.5g**
Sodium: **392mg**
Protein: **54g**
Fiber: **2.2g**
Sugars: **11g**

(if using all olive oil)

If you're like me and love a spicy tomato sauce, I've got a chicken dinner for you. *Fra Diavolo* is Italian for "Brother Devil," and the name is synonymous with heat. But don't worry: it's made with the perfect balance of spice so you'll be fully satisfied without feeling like you're breathing fire. This goes wonderfully over zoodles or spaghetti squash (see page 104).

Prep Time	Sauté Time	Pressure Building Time	Pressure Cook Time	Total Time
5 MIN	15 MIN	10–15 MIN	5 MIN	40 MIN

2 tablespoons extra-virgin olive oil

2 tablespoons ghee (store-bought or homemade, page 39) or additional olive oil

1 large Spanish or yellow onion, diced

1 green bell pepper, seeded and diced

3 cloves garlic, minced or pressed

3 pounds boneless, skinless chicken thighs and/or breasts, cut into bite-size pieces

2 cups canned no-salt-added crushed tomatoes

1 cup low-sodium chicken broth

¼–½ cup hot sauce (the hotter the sauce, the more diavolo!)

1 teaspoon seasoned salt

1 teaspoon Italian seasoning

1 teaspoon Old Bay seasoning (optional)

½ teaspoon cayenne pepper (optional)

½ teaspoon crushed red pepper flakes, plus more for serving (optional)

8–10 ounces cherry or grape tomatoes

5–8 ounces baby spinach

1 (6-ounce) can no-salt-added tomato paste

1 Add the oil and ghee to the Instant Pot, hit Sauté, and Adjust so it's on the More or High setting. Once the oil's bubbling and the ghee's melted (about 3 minutes), add the onion and bell pepper and sauté, stirring occasionally, for about 5 minutes, until slightly softened. Add the garlic and sauté for 1 minute.

2 Add the chicken and sauté for about 3 minutes, until it turns pinkish-white.

3 Add the crushed tomatoes, broth, hot sauce, seasoned salt, Italian seasoning, Old Bay (if using), cayenne (if using), and crushed red pepper flakes (if using). Stir until well combined.

4 Top with the fresh tomatoes and spinach but *do not stir* (don't worry if it comes to the brim of the pot—it'll cook down into nothing).

5 Secure the lid, move the valve to the sealing position, hit Keep Warm/Cancel, and then hit Manual or Pressure Cook on High Pressure for 5 minutes. Quick release when done.

6 Stir in the tomato paste and let rest for 5 minutes.

7 Serve topped with additional crushed red pepper flakes, if desired.

6

MEAT

Just because you're trying to eat healthier doesn't mean you need to sacrifice being a ravenous carnivore. As with everything else, red meat should be eaten in moderation, and it can be a great source of iron and protein. In this chapter we're going to make some of the most succulent meat dishes that you'll soon call your favorites.

= AIR FRYER LID   DF = DAIRY-FREE

K = KETO   GF = GLUTEN-FREE

P = PALEO   V = VEGETARIAN

+ = COMPLIANT WITH MODIFICATIONS   VN = VEGAN

FRENCH ONION POT ROAST

Serves 6

PER SERVING

Calories: **456**

Fat: **21.9g**

Carbs: **7.6g**

Sodium: **714mg**

Protein: **51.3g**

Fiber: **0.9g**

Sugars: **2.2g**

 K + *(if using sugar-free steak sauce and you don't mind a slurry)*

P + *(if using sugar-free steak sauce and you don't mind a slurry)*

GF

Picture French onion soup showering love all over a fork-tender, fall-apart roast: that's exactly what this dish is, and it's a meat lover's dream come true. It goes great with a bowl of Roasted Garlic & Spinach Soup (page 84).

Prep Time	Sauté Time	Pressure Building Time	Pressure Cook Time	Natural Release Time	Total Time
10 MIN	20 MIN	10–15 MIN	60 MIN	15 MIN	2 HRS

2 teaspoons black pepper

2 teaspoons dried thyme

2 teaspoons garlic salt

1 teaspoon seasoned salt

1 teaspoon onion powder

1 teaspoon garlic powder

1 (3-pound) chuck roast

3 tablespoons extra-virgin olive oil

4 teaspoons ghee (store-bought or homemade, page 39)

3 large onions (any kind), thinly sliced (I used 1 of each: Vidalia [sweet], red, and yellow)

3 cloves garlic, thinly sliced

2 tablespoons Worcestershire sauce or sugar-free steak sauce

1 cup low-sodium beef broth

1/2 cup dry red wine (like a cabernet) or additional broth

2 tablespoons cornstarch or arrowroot powder

2 tablespoons cold water

1 Mix together the pepper, thyme, garlic salt, seasoned salt, onion powder, and garlic powder and rub the mix into the roast on all sides.

2 Add the oil to the Instant Pot, hit Sauté, and Adjust so it's on the More or High setting. After 3 minutes of heating, sear the seasoned roast in the pot without moving it for 1–2 minutes on each side. Remove the roast from the pot and set aside.

3 Without wiping out the liner pot, add the ghee and, as it melts, use a wooden spoon to scrape up any spices stuck to the bottom. Add the onions and sauté for about 10 minutes, until fully softened and cooked down, continuing to occasionally stir and scrape up any browned bits.

CONTINUES

While most Instant Pot recipes keep the pressure cooking time the same even if you're doubling or halving recipes, roasts are an exception. Since roasts are thick, you'll need to adjust the cooking time per pound of meat. For this recipe, cook the roast for 60 minutes for 3 pounds, 70 minutes for 4 pounds, and 80 minutes for 5 pounds. Allow a 15-minute natural release regardless of the roast's size. But always use fresh (not frozen) meat for this recipe.

Cauliflower Aligot (page 236) makes the perfect companion to this French-style pot roast!

JEFF'S TIPS

  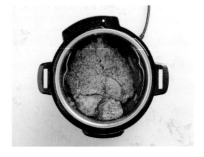

4 Add the garlic and Worcestershire or steak sauce and continue to stir and scrape for another minute, until the bottom of the pot is smooth.

5 Place the trivet on top of the onions with the handles facing upward, then pour in the broth and wine. Place the roast on top of the trivet, fat side up (so the juices will run through the meat as it cooks).

6 Secure the lid, move the valve to the sealing position, hit Keep Warm/Cancel, and then hit Manual or Pressure Cook on High Pressure for 60 minutes. When done, allow a 15-minute natural release followed by a quick release.

7 Carefully remove the roast and the trivet and let the meat rest on a cutting board.

8 Mix together the cornstarch and water to form a slurry.

9 Hit Keep Warm/Cancel, Sauté, and Adjust so it's on the More or High setting. Once bubbling, stir in the slurry and let bubble for 30–60 seconds, then hit Keep Warm/Cancel and keep it on the Keep Warm setting.

10 Slice the pot roast against the grain and add the slices to the sauce (still on the Keep Warm setting). Give everything a final stir, then serve.

STUFFED PEPPERS

Serves 4

PER SERVING
Calories: **355**
Fat: **18.5g**
Carbs: **21.8g**
Sodium: **358mg**
Protein: **27.6g**
Fiber: **5.6g**
Sugars: **11.8g**

K + *(if using sugar-free steak sauce)*
P + *(if using sugar-free steak sauce)*
DF
GF

Picture it: an entire bell pepper stuffed full of seasoned beef and rice and then cooked to sheer perfection. Not only is this dish super simple to make, it's even easier and quicker (but just as delish) since we use cauliflower in place of rice, making it a perfect healthy meal for a busy weeknight.

Prep Time	Sauté Time	Pressure Building Time	Pressure Cook Time	Optional Broiling Time	Total Time
10 MIN	15 MIN	10–15 MIN	4 MIN	1–2 MIN	45 MIN

2 tablespoons extra-virgin olive oil

1 pound 90% lean ground beef, ground turkey, or ground chicken

1 small yellow onion, diced

2 cloves garlic, minced or pressed

1 teaspoon seasoned salt

1 teaspoon garlic powder

1 teaspoon Italian seasoning

1 teaspoon dried oregano

2 tablespoons Worcestershire sauce or sugar-free steak sauce

1 (8-ounce) can no-salt-added tomato sauce (not the same as pasta sauce)

1 (6-ounce) can no-salt-added tomato paste

1 cup cauliflower rice (store-bought or homemade, see Jeff's Tips, page 177)

4 medium-size bell peppers (any color you wish), tops sliced off and ribs and seeds removed so they're hollowed out

½ cup shredded low-fat cheese of your choice, divided (optional)

1 Add the oil to the Instant Pot, hit Sauté, and Adjust so it's on the More or High setting. After 3 minutes of heating, add the ground beef and sauté, breaking it up with a spoon until it's crumbled and cooked through, about 5 minutes. Carefully skim off the juices from the liner pot with a serving spoon. (Alternatively, you can remove the liner pot and drain the contents in a fine-mesh strainer set over a bowl. Discard the juices in the bowl, return the meat to the liner pot, and place it back in the Instant Pot.)

2 Add the onion and sauté for 5 minutes, or until slightly softened. Add the garlic and sauté for 1 minute.

CONTINUES

3 Add the seasoned salt, garlic powder, Italian seasoning, and oregano and sauté for 1 minute.

4 Add the Worcestershire or steak sauce and deglaze the bottom of the pot, scraping up any browned bits. (If using sugar-free steak sauce, try to deglaze as well as possible.)

5 Add the tomato sauce, tomato paste, and cauliflower rice and stir until well combined. Hit Keep Warm/Cancel to turn off the pot.

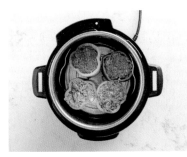

6 Scoop out the meat mixture and divide it evenly into the hollowed peppers. Rinse out the liner pot, pat dry, and return it to the Instant Pot.

7 Put the trivet in the pot, pour in 1 cup of water, and stand the stuffed peppers on the trivet. Place a sheet of aluminum foil over the peppers, leaving it open on the sides for the steam to build (NOTE: This is to prevent additional moisture from getting in the filling.)

8 Secure the lid, move the valve to the sealing position, and hit Manual or Pressure Cook on High Pressure for 4 minutes. Quick release when done and remove the foil.

9 Now you can either serve as is or top each pepper with 2 tablespoons shredded cheese. If topping with cheese, add the air fryer lid, hit Broil (400°F) for 1–2 minutes, and hit Start to begin. The cheese will be bubbly and brown, and it will be time to serve! (NOTE: You can also place the stuffed peppers on a foil-lined baking sheet, top with the cheese, and broil in the oven for 1–2 minutes, until the cheese is melted and bubbling.)

JEFF'S TIPS

To make fresh cauliflower rice, simply coarsely chop 1 head of cauliflower (stalk and greens removed) and pulse in a food processor until it's a rice-like consistency. Even easier, get a frozen bag from your grocery store, let it thaw, and squeeze dry with paper towels.

If you prefer regular rice to cauliflower rice, before Step 1, pressure cook ½ cup rice and ½ cup water for 3 minutes for white rice or 25 minutes for brown rice, then allow a 10-minute natural release followed by a quick release for either. This will increase the carbs by about 9g.

BEEF & BROCCOLI

Serves 6

PER SERVING
Calories: **578**
Fat: **35.5g**
Carbs: **17.5g**
Sodium: **431mg**
Protein: **43.7g**
Fiber: **2.1g**
Sugars: **4.7g**

Without question, Beef & Broccoli is one of the most popular and classic dishes in Chinese American cuisine. I wanted to try my own take for a lighter version that substitutes coconut aminos for soy sauce to cut down on the sodium and eliminate gluten. My popular, no-frills recipe also happens to be pretty light! Serve over rice (see page 114).

Prep Time	Sauté Time	Pressure Building Time	Pressure Cook Time	Natural Release Time	Total Time
10 MIN	8 MIN	10–15 MIN	10 MIN	15 MIN	55 MIN

¼ cup sesame oil

1 tablespoon Shaoxing wine or dry sherry

1 large white or yellow onion, diced

1 bunch scallions, sliced

3 cloves garlic, minced or pressed

1 cup low-sodium beef broth

¼ cup gluten-free hoisin sauce

¼ cup coconut aminos, low-sodium soy sauce, or tamari

2 tablespoons gluten-free oyster sauce

2 pounds flank steak, sliced against the grain into ¼-inch-thick strips

1–2 heads broccoli, cut into bite-size florets (or about 20 ounces frozen broccoli florets)

¼ cup cornstarch or arrowroot powder

¼ cup cold water

1 Combine the sesame oil and wine in the Instant Pot, hit Sauté, and Adjust so it's on the More or High setting. After 3 minutes of heating, add the onion and scallions and cook for 2 minutes, until slightly softened. Add the garlic and cook for 1 minute.

2 Add the broth, hoisin sauce, coconut aminos, and oyster sauce. Stir until well combined. Add the flank steak and stir to coat.

3 Secure the lid, move the valve to the sealing position, hit Keep Warm/Cancel, and then hit Manual or Pressure Cook on High Pressure for 10 minutes. When done, allow a 15-minute natural release followed by a quick release.

4 Meanwhile, put the broccoli florets in a microwave-safe bowl, add about ¼ inch of water, cover with plastic wrap, and microwave for 3–4 minutes, until tender (if frozen, microwave for 9–10 minutes). Drain.

5 Mix together the cornstarch and water to form a slurry.

6 Hit Keep Warm/Cancel, hit Sauté, and Adjust so it's on the More or High setting. Once bubbling, stir in the slurry, let bubble for 30 seconds, and then hit Keep Warm/Cancel to turn off the pot. The sauce will have thickened perfectly by now. Add the steamed broccoli and stir into the sauce, then serve.

JEFF'S TIP If you want the sauce a touch sweet, add 2 tablespoons pure maple syrup or raw honey in Step 2; this will increase the carbs by about 4.5g.

CRISPY CARNITAS

Serves 8

PER SERVING

Calories: **585**

Fat: **33g**

Carbs: **12.5g**

Sodium: **279mg**

Protein: **56.8g**

Fiber: **2.6g**

Sugars: **6.1g**

Carnitas refers to a citrus-infused, Mexican-style pork. Sometimes it's chunky, and sometimes it's shredded to resemble pulled pork. I go with the latter. It is *so* juicy and tender, and is simply amazing either right out of the pot or with a bit of a crisp at the end.

Prep Time	Pressure Building Time	Pressure Cook Time	Natural Release Time	Crisping Time	Total Time
15 MIN	**10–15** MIN	**60** MIN	**10** MIN	**12** MIN	**1 HR 50 MIN**

1 tablespoon onion powder

1 tablespoon garlic powder

1 tablespoon ground cumin

2 teaspoons seasoned salt

1½ teaspoons dried oregano

1 teaspoon black pepper

1 teaspoon chili powder

¼ teaspoon ground cinnamon

5 pounds boneless country-style ribs or boneless pork shoulder/butt, cut into 1–1½-inch strips (NOTE: If you can find only a bone-in pork butt/shoulder, just cook it whole, then remove the bone before you shred the meat—it should fall off easily.)

1 cup light beer or low-sodium chicken or beef broth

Juice of 2 oranges (about ½ cup)

Juice of 2 limes

6 cloves garlic, minced or pressed

1 large Spanish onion, peeled and quartered

¼–½ cup salsa (optional)

¼ cup taco sauce (optional)

Tortillas (any kind), warmed (optional)

1 Mix the onion powder, garlic powder, cumin, seasoned salt, oregano, pepper, chili powder, and cinnamon together until well blended. Rub the seasoning all over the pork strips.

2 Pour the beer or broth, orange juice, and lime juice into the Instant Pot and add the garlic; give it a stir. Place the onion quarters in the pot, round side down, and lay the pork strips on top of them. (If you have more pork than fits in one layer, place the second layer on top in a crisscross fashion.)

CONTINUES

3 Secure the lid, move the valve to the sealing position, and hit Manual or Pressure Cook on High Pressure for 60 minutes. When done, allow a 10-minute natural release followed by a quick release.

4 Use tongs to transfer the pork and onions to a large bowl (the pork will most likely fall apart, as it should). Reserve ¼–½ cup of the juices in the pot and discard (or freeze) the rest. If your pork has a bone, remove the meat and discard the bone.

5 You can now easily shred the pork and onion with a pair of forks. Pour the reserved juices over the shredded pork; you want to use enough so there's moisture but not so much that it's drowning.

6 Return the meat to the empty pot. Add the air fryer lid, hit Broil (400°F) for 8 minutes, and hit Start to begin. After 8 minutes, stir the meat from the bottom of the pot to the top and give it an additional 4 minutes on broil. The shredded pork should be about half crisp and half soft when done and mixed together. Alternatively, you can transfer the meat to a foil-lined baking sheet and broil it in the oven for 5–10 minutes, flipping once midway through (keep an eye on it, as ovens vary). Just be careful not to go for too long so you don't dry it out.

8 Transfer to a serving dish and serve on its own, in warm tortillas with your favorite toppings, or on a salad!

JEFF'S TIPS If you want even more citrus flavor, add the rinds of the oranges and limes on top of the pork in Step 2 and then discard after pressure cooking.

To make this paleo, use broth instead of beer (or use a light beer if you're okay with that). To make it keto, also skip the oranges.

7 If using the salsa and/or taco sauce, stir it into the meat.

BEEF BOURGUIGNON

A tip of the hat to Julia Child for introducing this dish to American kitchens. Beef Bourguignon is a magnificent French beef stew with a red wine base that relies on bacon for its flavor foundation (keto lovers, rejoice). If you perceive this as being too fancy or complex for a weeknight, don't be deterred—it's very simple to make in the Instant Pot while also making you feel like a seasoned pro!

Serves 8

PER SERVING
Calories: **578**
Fat: **27.3g**
Carbs: **13.9g**
Sodium: **743mg**
Protein: **60.4g**
Fiber: **2.1g**
Sugars: **5.3g**

 K⁺ *(if you don't mind a slurry)*

P⁺ *(if you don't mind a slurry)*

GF

Prep Time	Sauté Time	Pressure Building Time	Pressure Cook Time	Natural Release Time	Total Time
10 MIN	**13** MIN	**10–15** MIN	**20** MIN	**10** MIN	**1 HR 5 MIN**

- **3 tablespoons ghee (store-bought or homemade, page 39), divided**
- **6 strips thick-cut bacon *or* 8 ounces pancetta, cut into tiny pieces**
- **3 cloves garlic, minced or pressed**
- **1 pound baby bella mushrooms, sliced**
- **1 cup dry red wine (like a pinot noir) or additional broth**

- **3 pounds beef stew meat or chuck, cut into bite-size pieces**
- **1 cup low-sodium beef broth**
- **1 (6-ounce) can no-salt-added tomato paste, divided**
- **2 cups pearl onions, drained (Do *not* use cocktail onions. You can find frozen pearl onions in most markets, no need to thaw before adding.)**

- **1 teaspoon dried tarragon**
- **1 teaspoon dried thyme**
- **1 teaspoon seasoned salt**
- **1 teaspoon black pepper**
- **2 bay leaves**
- **2 tablespoons cornstarch or arrowroot powder**
- **2 tablespoons cold water**

1 Add 2 tablespoons of the ghee to the Instant Pot, hit Sauté, and Adjust so it's on the More or High setting. Once it's melted and bubbling (about 3 minutes), add the bacon and garlic and sauté for about 5 minutes, until the bacon begins to get slightly crispy, stirring occasionally. (It's okay if the bottom of the pot begins to look like it's burning. All of this will be deglazed later, and the flavor that's cooking up right now is key to the recipe!)

2 Add the mushrooms and remaining 1 tablespoon of ghee and sauté for 2 minutes.

3 Add the wine or broth and deglaze the bottom of the pot, getting up any browned bits. Let simmer for 1 minute.

CONTINUES

4 Add the beef, followed by the broth, 2 tablespoons of the tomato paste, pearl onions, tarragon, thyme, seasoned salt, and pepper. Top with the bay leaves.

5 Secure the lid, move the valve to the sealing position, hit Keep Warm/Cancel, and then hit the Manual or Pressure Cook button on High Pressure for 20 minutes. When done, allow a 10-minute natural release followed by a quick release.

6 Meanwhile, mix together the cornstarch and water to form a slurry.

7 Remove the bay leaves, hit Keep Warm/Cancel, and then hit Sauté again so it's on the More or High setting. Once it begins to bubble, stir in the slurry and let bubble for 30–60 seconds, then hit Keep Warm/Cancel again to turn off the pot. Once the bubbling dies down, stir in the remaining tomato paste until melded.

JEFF'S TIP If you want to go lighter than bacon, feel free to use turkey bacon or even tempeh, a meat substitute.

8 Transfer to a serving dish and serve.

SALT & VINEGAR PORK

Serves 6

PER SERVING
Calories: **512**
Fat: **30.8g**
Carbs: **8.7g**
Sodium: **154mg**
Protein: **44.6g**
Fiber: **0.6g**
Sugars: **1.1g**

 K + *(if using sweetener and you don't mind a slurry)*

 P + *(if you don't mind a slurry)*

 DF

GF

This dish is inspired by the classic and popular Filipino dish called adobo, a savory and tangy sauce that's usually draped over a protein. Soy sauce is normally the base for the sauce, but using coconut aminos in its place will cut down on some sodium, add additional flavor, and keep it naturally gluten-free. It is beyond simple to make and yields a very satisfying result. It goes wonderfully over any kind of rice (see page 114).

Prep Time	Sauté Time	Pressure Building Time	Pressure Cook Time	Natural Release Time	Total Time
10 MIN	10 MIN	10–15 MIN	15 MIN	5 MIN	50 MIN

2 tablespoons extra-virgin olive oil

1 large Spanish or yellow onion, diced

6 cloves garlic, minced or pressed

2½ pounds pork tenderloin, cut into bite-size pieces

¼ cup coconut aminos, low-sodium soy sauce, or tamari

¼ cup Garlic Broth (page 44) or low-sodium vegetable broth

¼ cup white vinegar

2 tablespoons apple cider vinegar

10 whole black peppercorns

1 tablespoon monk fruit sweetener or pure maple syrup

2 bay leaves

2 tablespoons cornstarch or arrowroot powder

2 tablespoons cold water

2 tablespoons raw honey (optional)

1 Add the oil to the Instant Pot, hit Sauté, and Adjust so it's on the More or High setting. After 3 minutes of heating, add the onion and sauté, stirring occasionally, for about 3 minutes, until slightly softened. Add the garlic and sauté for 2 minutes.

2 Add the pork and sauté for about 2 minutes, until it turns pinkish-white.

3 Add the coconut aminos, broth, white vinegar, apple cider vinegar, peppercorns, and sweetener or maple syrup. Stir well and top with the bay leaves.

4 Secure the lid, move the valve to the sealing position, and hit the Manual or Pressure Cook on High Pressure for 15 minutes. When done, allow a 5-minute natural release followed by a quick release.

5 Meanwhile, mix together the cornstarch and water to form a slurry.

6 Remove the bay leaves, hit Keep Warm/Cancel, hit Sauté again, and Adjust so it's on the More or High setting. Once it begins to bubble, stir in the slurry and let bubble for 30–60 seconds, then hit Keep Warm/Cancel again to turn off the pot.

7 Once the bubbling dies down, stir in the honey (if using), transfer to a serving dish, and serve.

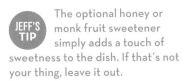

JEFF'S TIP The optional honey or monk fruit sweetener simply adds a touch of sweetness to the dish. If that's not your thing, leave it out.

MOROCCAN BEEF TAGINE

Serves 6

PER SERVING
Calories: **494**
Fat: **20.1g**
Carbs: **17.1g**
Sodium: **314mg**
Protein: **53.1g**
Fiber: **2.7g**
Sugars: **8g**

K ⁺ (if using sweetener and you don't mind a slurry)

P ⁺ (if you don't mind a slurry)

DF

GF

Be sure to load up *Casablanca* on the small screen tonight, because you've got a date with the perfect beef dish to complement it. Tagine is a Moroccan dish that is full of deep and rich exotic flavor, but with ingredients that are local to any market. It's traditionally served over couscous, but you could also use rice or quinoa (see page 54). This recipe will have you staring lovingly at your plate and whispering, "Here's looking at you, kid."

Prep Time	Sauté Time	Pressure Building Time	Pressure Cook Time	Natural Release Time	Total Time
10 MIN	12 MIN	10–15 MIN	20 MIN	10 MIN	1 HR 5 MIN

3 tablespoons extra-virgin olive oil

1 medium yellow onion, diced

1 large carrot, peeled and sliced into ¼-inch disks

3 cloves garlic, minced or pressed

1 tablespoon minced or grated ginger

3 pounds beef stew meat or chuck meat, cut into bite-size pieces

1 cup dry red wine (like a pinot noir) or additional broth

1 cup low-sodium beef broth

1½ teaspoons ground allspice

1 teaspoon ground cinnamon

1 teaspoon curry powder

1 teaspoon seasoned salt

1 teaspoon black pepper

2 tablespoons cornstarch or arrowroot powder

2 tablespoons cold water

1 tablespoon raw honey or monk fruit sweetener

1 (6-ounce) can no-salt-added tomato paste

1 Add the oil to the Instant Pot, hit Sauté, and Adjust so it's on the More or High setting. After 3 minutes of heating, add the onion and carrot and sauté for about 5 minutes, until slightly softened. Add the garlic and ginger and sauté for 2 minutes.

2 Add the beef and cook, stirring occasionally, until very lightly browned, about 2 minutes.

3 Add the wine, broth, allspice, cinnamon, curry powder, seasoned salt, and pepper and stir well.

4 Secure the lid, move the valve to the sealing position, hit Keep Warm/Cancel, and then hit the Manual or Pressure Cook button on High Pressure for 20 minutes. When done, allow a 10-minute natural release followed by a quick release.

5 Mix together the cornstarch and water to form a slurry.

6 Hit Keep Warm/Cancel, hit Sauté, and Adjust so it's on the More or High setting. Once it begins to bubble, stir in the slurry and let bubble for 30–60 seconds, then hit Keep Warm/Cancel to turn off the pot. Once the bubbling dies down, stir in the honey or sweetener and tomato paste until melded.

7 Transfer to a serving dish and serve.

JEFF'S TIP

Some people enjoy tossing some dried apricots and/or raisins (dark or golden) into this dish. Feel free to do so in Step 6 after adding the honey and tomato paste, just before serving.

CHICAGO-STYLE ITALIAN BEEF

Serves 8

PER SERVING
Calories: **578**
Fat: **35g**
Carbs: **8.8g**
Sodium: **582mg**
Protein: **54.2g**
Fiber: **1.4g**
Sugars: **4.2g**

 (if using sugar-free steak sauce and monk fruit sweetener)

 (if using sugar-free steak sauce)

If you love a Mississippi Pot Roast—the hugely popular Instant Pot braised beef made with seasoning packets and pepperoncini—try this version, which takes the idea to Chicago. Equally as tangy, with an unbelievable melt-in-your-mouth finish, this roast is going to make you the host with the most. Don't worry, the pepperoncini don't make it spicy; they just provide a taste as thrilling as a view from the Sears (sorry, Willis) Tower. If you like, serve in whole-wheat hero rolls or buns (or be decadent and use a nice loaf of Italian bread).

Prep Time	Sauté Time	Pressure Building Time	Pressure Cook Time	Natural Release Time	Total Time
10 MIN	10 MIN	10–15 MIN	60 MIN	15 MIN	1 HR 45 MIN

- **6 tablespoons extra-virgin olive oil, divided**
- **1 large red onion, cut into thin wedges**
- **3 large green bell peppers, seeded and sliced into ¼-inch-thick strips**
- **3 cloves garlic, minced or pressed**
- **¼ cup red wine vinegar or white vinegar**
- **1 cup low-sodium beef broth**

- **1 tablespoon Worcestershire sauce or sugar-free steak sauce**
- **1 (16-ounce) jar pepperoncini or banana peppers (or a mix of the two), drained, ¼ cup juice reserved** (NOTE: These won't make the dish spicy once they're cooked. The peppers magically transform into a rich flavor for the gravy—so make sure you add them!)

- **1 tablespoon pure maple syrup or monk fruit sweetener**
- **1 teaspoon seasoned salt**
- **1 teaspoon garlic powder**
- **½ teaspoon dried oregano**
- **½ teaspoon Italian seasoning**
- **1 (3-pound) chuck roast**
- **1 (16-ounce) jar giardiniera (pickled veggies), drained, for topping (optional)**

 JEFF'S TIPS

The sauce is meant to be thin, but if you want it thicker, mix together 2–4 tablespoons cornstarch or arrowroot powder with 2–4 tablespoons cold water to form a slurry (the more, the thicker). Hit Keep Warm/Cancel, hit Sauté, and Adjust so it's on the More or High setting. Once bubbling, stir in the slurry and let bubble for 30–60 seconds, then hit Keep Warm/Cancel to turn off the pot. The sauce will then thicken into more of a gravy-like consistency.

While most Instant Pot recipes keep the pressure cooking time the same even if you're doubling or halving recipes, roasts are an exception. Since roasts are thick, you'll need to adjust the cooking time per pound of meat. For this recipe, cook the roast for 60 minutes for 3 pounds, 70 minutes for 4 pounds, or 80 minutes for 5 pounds. Allow a 15-minute natural release regardless of the roast's size. Always use fresh (not frozen) meat for this recipe.

CONTINUES

1 Add 3 tablespoons of the oil to the Instant Pot, hit Sauté, and Adjust so it's on the More or High setting. After 3 minutes of heating, add the onion and bell peppers and sauté, stirring occasionally, for about 5 minutes, until slightly softened. Add the garlic and sauté for 1 minute.

2 Add the vinegar and scrape the bottom of the pot to loosen any browned bits. Add the remaining 3 tablespoons of oil, broth, Worcestershire or steak sauce, pepperoncini juice (but not the peppers yet), maple syrup or sweetener, seasoned salt, garlic powder, oregano, and Italian seasoning. Give everything a stir until combined.

3 Place the trivet on top of the onion and bell peppers with the handles facing upward. Place the roast on top of the trivet, fat side up (so the juices will run through the meat as it cooks). Top with the pepperoncini.

5 Remove the roast and the trivet and let the meat rest on a cutting board.

4 Secure the lid, move the valve to the sealing position, hit Keep Warm/ Cancel, and then hit Manual or Pressure Cook on High Pressure for 60 minutes. When done, allow a 15-minute natural release followed by a quick release.

6 Slice the pot roast against the grain and add the slices to the sauce (still on the Keep Warm setting). Give everything a final stir, then serve topped with giardiniera, if desired.

CUBAN PICADILLO CHILI

Serves 6

PER SERVING
Calories: **387**
Fat: **21.2g**
Carbs: **23.5g**
Sodium: **742mg**
Protein: **25.9g**
Fiber: **4.9g**
Sugars: **13.4g**

K + *(if using sugar-free steak sauce)*
P + *(if using sugar-free steak sauce)*
DF
GF

Some would argue that picadillo, a classic Cuban dish enlivened with simple yet powerful spices, is the original chili or Sloppy Joe, and I can see why. Loaded with ground beef, it typically employs a few super flavorful ingredients such as raisins, olives, and almonds to keep it interesting and unique, yet simple to prepare. It is a truly delicious dish, and I decided to give this version a bit of a chili-like flair.

Prep Time	Sauté Time	Pressure Building Time	Pressure Cook Time	Total Time
10 MIN	15 MIN	10–15 MIN	4 MIN	40 MIN

- 2 tablespoons extra-virgin olive oil
- 1½ pounds 90% lean ground beef
- 1 medium Vidalia (sweet) onion, diced
- 1 large red bell pepper, seeded and diced
- 3 cloves garlic, minced or pressed
- 2 teaspoons ground cumin
- 1 teaspoon seasoned salt
- 1 teaspoon garlic powder
- 1 teaspoon chili powder
- 1 teaspoon dried oregano
- ¼ teaspoon ground cinnamon
- 2 tablespoons Worcestershire sauce or sugar-free steak sauce
- ½ cup low-sodium beef broth
- 1 (8-ounce) can no-salt-added tomato sauce (not the same as pasta sauce)
- 1 (14.5-ounce) can no-salt-added diced tomatoes, with their juices
- 1 tablespoon red wine vinegar
- 1 (6-ounce) can no-salt-added tomato paste
- ½ cup green olives (any kind), pitted and either sliced or kept whole, plus more for topping
- ½ cup sugar-free raisins, plus more for topping (optional)
- 1 tablespoon capers (optional)
- ¼ cup raw almonds, slivered, plus more for topping (optional)

1 Add the oil to the Instant Pot, hit Sauté, and Adjust so it's on the More or High setting. After 3 minutes of heating, add the ground beef and sauté, breaking it up with a spoon until it's crumbled and cooked through, about 5 minutes. Carefully skim off the juices from the liner pot with a serving spoon. (Alternatively, you can remove the liner pot and drain the contents in a fine-mesh strainer set over a bowl. Discard the juices in the bowl, return the meat to the liner pot, and place it back in the Instant Pot.)

2 Add the onion and bell pepper and sauté for 5 minutes, or until slightly softened. Add the garlic and sauté for 1 minute.

CONTINUES

3 Add the cumin, seasoned salt, garlic powder, chili powder, oregano, and cinnamon and sauté for 1 minute.

4 Add the Worcestershire or steak sauce and deglaze the bottom of the pot, loosening any browned bits. (If using sugar-free steak sauce, try to deglaze as well as possible.)

5 Add the broth, tomato sauce, diced tomatoes, and vinegar and stir until well combined.

6 Secure the lid, move the valve to the sealing position, hit Keep Warm/Cancel, and then hit Manual or Pressure Cook on High Pressure for 4 minutes. Quick release when done.

7 Add the tomato paste, olives, raisins (if using), capers (if using), and almonds (if using). Stir until the tomato paste is melded into the sauce. Let rest and thicken for 5 minutes, then serve topped with additional olives, raisins, and almonds, if desired.

JEFF'S TIP

If using the almonds, feel free to toast them prior to serving for some additional flavor.

SRIRACHA-SCALLION STEAK

Serves 6

PER SERVING
Calories: **479**
Fat: **25.6g**
Carbs: **16.2g**
Sodium: **358mg**
Protein: **43.5g**
Fiber: **2.2g**
Sugars: **4.7g**

K + *(if you don't mind a slurry)*

P + *(if you don't mind a slurry)*

DF

GF

On the day of a windy storm, I had no intention of shopping for ingredients but instead planned to use whatever I found in my fridge. I spied flank steak, scallions, and sriracha. Alliteration aside, it immediately became a no-brainer to combine them. Sriracha takes this dish to the spicier side, but the heat is slightly offset by the cool crisp of some scintillating scallions. A zesty masterpiece awaits. Serve over rice (see page 114).

Prep Time	Sauté Time	Pressure Building Time	Pressure Cook Time	Natural Release Time	Total Time
5 MIN	8 MIN	10–15 MIN	10 MIN	15 MIN	50 MIN

¼ cup sesame oil

1 large white or yellow onion, diced

2 red bell peppers, seeded and diced

2 bunches scallions, cut into 1-inch pieces, divided

6 cloves garlic, thinly sliced

2 pounds flank steak, cut against the grain into ¼-inch-thick, 2–3-inch-long strips

1 cup low-sodium beef broth

¼ cup coconut aminos, low-sodium soy sauce, or tamari

2 tablespoons sriracha

1 tablespoon chili-garlic sauce (usually found in the market next to the sriracha; it comes in a small plastic container)

¼ teaspoon crushed red pepper flakes (optional)

3 tablespoons cornstarch or arrowroot powder

3 tablespoons cold water

1 Add the oil to the Instant Pot, hit Sauté, and Adjust so it's on the More or High setting. After 3 minutes of heating, add the onion, bell peppers, and half the scallions and cook for 2 minutes, until slightly softened. Add the garlic and sauté for 1 minute.

2 Add the flank steak and sauté, stirring until the edges are lightly browned but not fully cooked, about 2 minutes.

3 Add the broth, coconut aminos, sriracha, chili-garlic sauce, and crushed red pepper flakes (if using) and stir until well combined.

5 Mix together the cornstarch and water to form a slurry.

4 Secure the lid, move the valve to the sealing position, hit Keep Warm/Cancel, and then hit Manual or Pressure Cook on High Pressure for 10 minutes. When done, allow a 15-minute natural release followed by a quick release.

6 Hit Keep Warm/Cancel and then hit Sauté. Once bubbling, stir in the slurry, let bubble for 30–60 seconds, and then hit Keep Warm/Cancel again to turn off the pot. The sauce will have thickened perfectly by now. Add the remaining scallions, stir into the sauce, and serve.

JEFF'S TIP Want it even spicier? Add another tablespoon of chili-garlic sauce. If you can't find chili-garlic sauce, just use up to another tablespoon of sriracha.

HONEY-GARLIC PORK TENDERLOIN

Serves 6

PER SERVING
Calories: **333**
Fat: **6g**
Carbs: **34.1g**
Sodium: **655mg**
Protein: **32.5g**
Fiber: **0.9g**
Sugars: **9.8g**

 + *(if you don't mind a slurry)*

 DF

GF

Of course I had to end the meat chapter on a sweet and porky note. Honey and garlic play very nicely together over pork tenderloin medallions in a recipe so irresistible, it will become a regular in your rotation.

Prep Time	Marinating Time	Pressure Building Time	Pressure Cook Time	Natural Release Time	Total Time
5 MIN	8–24 HRS	10–15 MIN	8 MIN	10 MIN	8½ HRS

THE MARINADE

½ cup low-sodium beef broth

2 tablespoons pure maple syrup

2 tablespoons coconut aminos, low-sodium soy sauce, or tamari

2 tablespoons balsamic vinegar

1 tablespoon Shaoxing wine or dry sherry

1 tablespoon gluten-free hoisin sauce (optional)

2 teaspoons kosher salt

1 teaspoon Chinese five-spice powder

½ teaspoon paprika

5 cloves garlic, minced or pressed

1 tablespoon minced or grated ginger

THE PORK

2 pounds pork tenderloin (*not* pork loin), sliced into 1-inch-thick medallions

THE SAUCE

½ cup low-sodium beef broth

¼ cup gluten-free hoisin sauce (optional)

2 tablespoons balsamic vinegar

½ teaspoon Chinese five-spice powder

5 cloves garlic, thinly sliced

3 tablespoons cornstarch or arrowroot powder

3 tablespoons cold water

⅓ cup raw honey

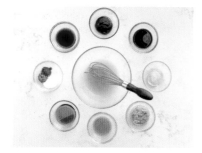

1 To make the marinade, whisk together all the marinade ingredients in a large bowl.

2 Put the pork medallions in a gallon-size ziplock bag, pour the marinade over them, and seal the bag, pressing all the air out. Refrigerate for 8–24 hours (the longer the better), flipping once midway through.

3 When ready to cook, empty the bag with the pork and all of its marinade into the Instant Pot. Add the broth, hoisin sauce, vinegar, Chinese five-spice, and garlic. Mix well and make sure the pork is mostly submerged in the sauce (it is fine if some of the pork protrudes above it).

4 Secure the lid, move the valve to the sealing position, and hit Manual or Pressure Cook on High Pressure for 8 minutes. Allow a 10-minute natural release followed by a quick release.

5 Mix together the cornstarch and water to form a slurry.

6 Use a slotted spoon to transfer the pork to a serving dish. (NOTE: If there's any foam, remove the liner pot and carefully pour the sauce through a fine-mesh strainer into a bowl. Allow the strainer to catch the excess fat from the pork, return the strained sauce to the liner pot, and place the liner pot back in the Instant Pot. Discard the fat in the strainer.)

7 Hit Keep Warm/Cancel, hit Sauté, and Adjust to the More or High setting. Add the slurry and stir well. Allow the sauce to bubble for 30–60 seconds, then hit Keep Warm/Cancel and allow it to simmer so it's only slightly bubbling. Add the honey and give it a good stir. The sauce will begin to thicken to that perfect consistency.

8 Using a serving spoon, drizzle the sauce over the pork and serve.

 JEFF'S TIP This goes nicely over Cilantro-Lime Basmati Rice (page 130).

7

SEAFOOD

Get ready to feel like you're sitting on
the dock of a bay in New England or overlooking
Italy's Amalfi coast. Treasures of the sea await
that are as easy to make as they are tasty. You'll
fall for them all—hook, line, and sinker.

≋ = AIR FRYER LID   DF = DAIRY-FREE

K = KETO   GF = GLUTEN-FREE

P = PALEO   V = VEGETARIAN

+ = COMPLIANT WITH MODIFICATIONS   VN = VEGAN

BOUILLABAISSE

A seafood lover's dream, French bouillabaisse is a hearty, tomato-based seafood stew with a variety of goodies tossed in. It is virtually identical to Italian cioppino with the addition of one game-changing ingredient: saffron.

Serves 8

PER SERVING
Calories: **236**
Fat: **8.3g**
Carbs: **7.6g**
Sodium: **690mg**
Protein: **35.3g**
Fiber: **1.2g**
Sugars: **3.1g**

K
P
DF
GF

Prep Time	Sauté Time	Pressure Building Time	Pressure Cook Time	Total Time
15 MIN	10 MIN	10–15 MIN	3 MIN	40 MIN

THE BASE

3 tablespoons extra-virgin olive oil

½ cup finely chopped leek (tender inner stalks only)

4 cups low-sodium vegetable broth

1 (28-ounce) can crushed tomatoes

⅓ cup dry sherry

Juice of ½ lemon

2 teaspoons seasoned salt

1 teaspoon dried basil

1 teaspoon dried parsley

½ teaspoon Old Bay seasoning

½ teaspoon saffron (expensive, so it's optional—but it's worth the purchase!)

1 bay leaf

THE SEAFOOD

1 pound cod, cut into bite-size pieces (or sub any mild white fish you prefer, such as haddock, red snapper, porgy, or striped bass)

1 pound raw large or jumbo shrimp, peeled and deveined

½ pound fresh scallops (any size)

½ pound fresh lump crabmeat (any kind)

1 tablespoon unsweetened nondairy milk

1 Add the olive oil to the Instant Pot, hit Sauté, and Adjust so it's on the More or High setting. After 3 minutes of heating, add the leek and sauté until browned and crispy, 3–5 minutes (NOTE: Keep a close eye on the pot—leeks can go from browned to burned very quickly.)

2 Add the broth, crushed tomatoes, sherry, lemon juice, seasoned salt, basil, parsley, Old Bay, saffron (if using), and bay leaf and stir well.

3 Secure the lid, move the valve to the sealing position, hit Keep Warm/Cancel, and then hit Manual or Pressure Cook on High Pressure for 3 minutes. Quick release when done.

4 Once the lid's off, "fish" out the bay leaf with a slotted spoon. Hit Keep Warm/Cancel, hit Sauté, and Adjust so it's on the Normal or Medium setting. Once bubbling, add the cod and let it cook for 2 minutes. Next, add the shrimp and scallops and cook for 2 minutes. Finally, add the crabmeat and milk and stir for 1 minute, then hit Keep Warm/Cancel.

5 Ladle into bowls and enjoy.

 JEFF'S TIP Want it a bit spicy? Add ½–1 teaspoon Zatarain's Concentrated Shrimp & Crab Boil in Step 4, along with the crabmeat and milk.

CRAB LEGS WITH GARLIC GHEE SAUCE

Serves 6

PER SERVING
with/without sauce

Calories: **255/178**

Fat: **11g/2.7g**

Carbs: **0.4g/0g**

Sodium: **1063mg/1050mg**

Protein: **35.9g/35.7g**

Fiber: **0g/0g**

Sugars: **0g/0g**

K

GF

What could be better than cracking into a crab leg to be rewarded with that sweet, succulent crabmeat? Well, I'd say dipping it in garlic ghee sauce is a pretty sure bet. This dish is just begging to be made on a lazy summer day.

Prep Time	Pressure Building Time	Pressure Cook Time	Total Time
5 MIN	**5–10** MIN	**2** MIN	**15** MIN

THE LEGS

1 tablespoon Zatarain's Concentrated Shrimp & Crab Boil (optional) (NOTE: This is going to make the broth quite spicy but it's simply to infuse the crab legs with flavor as they cook. You can reduce the amount to as low as 1 teaspoon or leave it out completely if you wish.)

4 pounds (4 sections/clusters) snow crab legs (thawed for 30 minutes in the sink if frozen)

Lemon wedges, for serving (optional)

THE GARLIC GHEE SAUCE

¼ cup ghee (store-bought or homemade, page 39)

2 cloves garlic, minced

½ teaspoon dried parsley

¼ teaspoon Old Bay seasoning

1 teaspoon grated Parmesan cheese

1 Pour 1 cup of water into the Instant Pot, add the Zatarain's (if using), and stir.

2 Place the trivet in the pot and rest the crab legs on it, maneuvering them so the lid can shut.

3 Secure the lid, move the valve to the sealing position, and hit Manual or Pressure Cook on High Pressure for 2 minutes. Quick release when done.

JEFF'S TIPS If you want a more intense garlic flavor, you can add ¼ teaspoon of Garlic Better Than Bouillon to the garlic ghee sauce in Step 4; this will increase the sodium by about 30mg.

Make it paleo by leaving out the Parmesan in the sauce.

4 While the pot is releasing its steam, make the garlic ghee dipping sauce. Put the ghee in a microwave-safe bowl and microwave for 10–15 seconds, until it's totally melted. Stir in the garlic, parsley, Old Bay, and Parmesan.

5 Transfer the crab legs to a plate and get crackin' and dippin'! Squeeze some fresh lemon on too if you'd like!

SHRIMP WITH LOBSTER SAUCE

Serves 6

PER SERVING
Calories: **180**
Fat: **1.6g**
Carbs: **10g**
Sodium: **511mg**
Protein: **27.3g**
Fiber: **1.4g**
Sugars: **2.8g**

This is probably my favorite shrimp dish to make in the Instant Pot—not only is it light while feeling rich, it's also done quickly. The delicate notes of lobster broth with a sweet and savory blend of spices and natural ingredients really send it home. You can find lobster broth near the chicken broth in most markets or you can use 1½ teaspoons Lobster Better Than Bouillon plus 1½ cups water—or see Jeff's Tips.

Prep Time	Pressure Building Time	Pressure Cook Time	Sauté Time	Total Time
10 MIN	5-10 MIN	O MIN	1 MINUTE	20 MIN

1½ cups lobster broth

1½ teaspoons coconut aminos, low-sodium soy sauce, or tamari

1½ teaspoons Shaoxing wine or dry sherry

1 teaspoon pure maple syrup or monk fruit sweetener

2 cloves garlic, minced or pressed

1½ teaspoons minced or grated ginger

½ teaspoon ground white pepper

1½ pounds raw large or jumbo shrimp, peeled and deveined

2 tablespoons cornstarch or arrowroot powder

2 tablespoons cold water

2 large egg whites

1½ cups frozen peas

1 bunch scallions, sliced

1½ teaspoons unsweetened nondairy milk

1 Combine the broth, coconut aminos, wine, maple syrup, garlic, ginger, and white pepper in the Instant Pot and stir well.

2 Add the shrimp and give it another stir. Secure the lid, move the valve to the sealing position, and hit Manual or Pressure Cook on High Pressure for O (yes, zero) minutes. (If using frozen shrimp, set for 1 minute.) Quick release when done.

3 Mix together the cornstarch and water to form a slurry. In another bowl, beat the egg whites.

4 Use a slotted spoon to transfer the shrimp to a serving dish.

5 Hit Keep Warm/Cancel, hit Sauté, and Adjust so it's on the More or High setting. As the broth is heating up, add the frozen peas and scallions (reserve a few for garnish), and stir. Once it begins to bubble, add the slurry and stir immediately as it bubbles for 30 seconds. Turn off the heat and let it cool down a bit—the broth is going to thicken into a sauce here.

6 Once the bubbles have mostly died down, add the beaten egg whites and stir immediately. Watch the magic happen as the sauce begins to transform!

7 Lastly, add the milk, stir, and *presto!*—the sauce is done. Spoon it over the shrimp in the serving dish, top with the reserved scallions, and serve.

JEFF'S TIPS If you don't have or don't feel like buying Lobster Better Than Bouillon or lobster broth, you can use low-sodium chicken or beef broth instead (but then it won't have that hint of lobster flavor).

To make the dish keto or paleo, simply leave out the peas.

PESTO SALMON

Serves 4

PER SERVING
Calories: **519**
Fat: **37.4g**
Carbs: **2.3g**
Sodium: **264mg**
Protein: **46.2g**
Fiber: **0.4g**
Sugars: **0.3g**

I'm obsessed with pesto sauce and love to pair it with a juicy, flaky salmon fillet. As delicious as it is, it's also super fast to make. I'm partial to serving it over zoodles (zucchini noodles)!

Prep Time	Pressure Building Time	Pressure Cook Time	Total Time
5 MIN	5–10 MIN	4 MIN	15 MIN

THE SALMON

4 (1-inch-thick) salmon fillets, skin on or off

Coconut aminos, low-sodium soy sauce, or tamari, for brushing on the salmon

THE PESTO

1½ cups loosely packed fresh basil leaves

3 cloves garlic, lightly smashed

½ cup grated Parmesan cheese

⅓ cup extra-virgin olive oil; or 1 ripe avocado, peeled and pitted, plus 2 tablespoons cold water

¼ cup pine nuts, raw cashews, walnuts, almonds, or shelled pistachio nuts

1 Place the trivet in the Instant Pot and pour in 1 cup of water. Place a parchment round on the trivet and lay the salmon on the parchment (it's okay if the fillets rest on each other).

2 Lightly brush coconut aminos on the top of each salmon fillet.

3 Secure the lid, move the valve to the sealing position, and hit Manual or Pressure Cook on High Pressure for 4 minutes. Quick release when done.

4 Meanwhile, make the pesto by combining all the ingredients in a food processor or blender and pureeing until it reaches the consistency you desire.

5 When done cooking, carefully remove the trivet and rest the salmon on a plate. Brush the pesto on each fillet and serve.

JEFF'S TIP If you're using frozen salmon fillets, increase the pressure cooking time to 6 minutes.

LOBSTER CREOLE

Inspired by Creole cooking, which relies on the use of tomatoes, this dish features the Big Easy "holy trinity" base (celery, onion, and bell pepper) and boasts similar flavors to a gumbo. It's incredibly easy to make, and the flavor payoff is beyond astounding. I use lobster as the star, but you can just as easily sub langostino meat (similar to crawfish) or shrimp (see Jeff's Tip). Either way, serve with rice (see page 114).

Serves 6

PER SERVING
Calories: **350**
Fat: **13.8g**
Carbs: **12.7g**
Sodium: **836mg**
Protein: **42.4g**
Fiber: **2.2g**
Sugars: **2.6g**

K + *(if using sugar-free steak sauce and you're okay with a slurry)*

P + *(if using sugar-free steak sauce and you're okay with a slurry)*

DF + *(if using olive oil)*

GF

Prep Time	Sauté Time	Pressure Building Time	Pressure Cook Time	Total Time
5 MIN	10 MIN	5–10 MIN	2 MIN	25 MIN

- ¼ cup ghee (store-bought or homemade, page 39) or extra-virgin olive oil
- 1 large shallot, diced
- 1 green bell pepper, seeded and diced
- 1 bunch scallions, sliced
- 1 rib celery, diced
- 3 cloves garlic, minced or pressed

- 2 cups lobster broth (I use 2 teaspoons Lobster Better Than Bouillon plus 2 cups water) or low-sodium vegetable broth
- 1 can no-salt-added diced tomatoes, with their juices
- Juice of ½ lemon
- 1 tablespoon hot sauce (optional)
- 1 teaspoon Worcestershire sauce or sugar-free steak sauce
- 2 teaspoons Creole, Cajun, or Louisiana seasoning (I like Tony Chachere's)

- 1 teaspoon seasoned salt
- 1 teaspoon paprika
- 1 teaspoon Old Bay seasoning
- ½ teaspoon Zatarain's Concentrated Shrimp & Crab Boil or cayenne pepper (optional)
- 2 pounds fresh or thawed frozen lobster tails
- 2 tablespoons cornstarch or arrowroot powder
- 2 tablespoons cold water

1 Add the ghee or olive oil to the Instant Pot, hit Sauté, and Adjust so it's on the More or High setting. Once it's melted and bubbling (about 3 minutes), add the shallot, bell pepper, scallions (reserve a few for garnish), and celery and sauté, stirring occasionally, for about 3 minutes. Add the garlic and sauté for 1 minute.

2 Add the broth, tomatoes, lemon juice, hot sauce (if using), Worcestershire or steak sauce, Creole seasoning, seasoned salt, paprika, Old Bay, and Zatarain's (if using) and stir until well combined.

CONTINUES

3 Place the trivet in the pot and lay the lobster tails, shell side down, on it. Secure the lid, move the valve to the sealing position, hit Keep Warm/Cancel, and then hit Manual or Pressure Cook on High Pressure for 2 minutes. Quick release when done, hit Keep Warm/Cancel to turn off the pot, and immediately remove the trivet and transfer the lobsters to an ice bath (a large bowl filled with cold water and ice cubes) to stop the cooking.

4 Once slightly cooled (about 3 minutes), place the lobster tails, shell side down, on a cutting board and use kitchen shears to cut the "vertebrae" of the tails down the center. Remove the meat from the shells and chop it up into bite-size pieces.

JEFF'S TIP Don't feel like "shelling" out for lobster? I gotcha! You can use 1½ pounds of langostino meat or shrimp (peeled and deveined) instead. The only difference is we won't be doing any pressure cooking here, just sautéing, so we don't overcook this seafood and give it a rubbery texture. In this case, you'd skip Steps 3 and 4 and simply add the langostino meat and/or shrimp at the end of Step 2 and cook until opaque, with the shrimp curled and cooked through (3–5 minutes).

5 Mix together the cornstarch and water to form a slurry. Hit Sauté and Adjust so it's on the More or High Setting. Once bubbling, add the slurry and let bubble for 30 seconds before hitting Keep Warm/Cancel to turn off the pot.

6 Return the lobster meat to the pot and stir until combined. Serve, garnished with the reserved scallions.

TILAPIA PICCATA

Serves 4

PER SERVING
Calories: **504**
Fat: **28.3g**
Carbs: **12.5g**
Sodium: **577mg**
Protein: **51g**
Fiber: **1g**
Sugars: **3.1g**

K + *(if using nondairy milk and you're okay with a slurry)*

GF

Lemon-butter sauce and tender fillets of mild white fish is a pairing that truly cannot be argued with. Once you try this Tilapia Piccata, it will quickly enter your rotation of healthy dinners.

Prep Time	Sauté Time	Pressure Building Time	Pressure Cook Time	Total Time
5 MIN	7 MIN	5–10 MIN	5 MIN	25 MIN

4 (1-inch-thick) skinless tilapia fillets

Lemon pepper seasoning, for rubbing on the tilapia

¼ cup extra-virgin olive oil

2 large shallots, diced

3 cloves garlic, minced or pressed

1½ cups Garlic Broth (page 44) or low-sodium chicken broth

1½ tablespoons cornstarch or arrowroot powder

1½ tablespoons cold water

1 tablespoon ghee (store-bought or homemade, page 39)

½ cup fat-free half-and-half or unsweetened nondairy milk

Juice of 2 lemons

⅓ cup grated Parmesan cheese

1 teaspoon dried parsley

1 tablespoon capers, plus more for topping (optional)

1 Lightly rub the tilapia fillets with some lemon pepper seasoning. Set aside.

2 Add the oil to the Instant Pot, hit Sauté, and Adjust so it's on the More or High setting. After 3 minutes of heating, add the shallots and sauté, stirring occasionally, for about 3 minutes, until slightly softened. Add the garlic and sauté for 1 minute.

CONTINUES

3 Place the trivet in the pot and pour in the broth. Place a parchment round on the trivet and lay the tilapia on the parchment (it's okay if the fillets rest on each other).

4 Secure the lid, move the valve to the sealing position, hit Keep Warm/Cancel, and then hit Manual or Pressure Cook on High Pressure for 5 minutes. Quick release when done. Remove the trivet carefully and place the tilapia in a serving dish.

5 Mix together the cornstarch and water to form a slurry.

6 Hit Keep Warm/Cancel, hit Sauté, and Adjust so it's on the More or High setting. Once bubbling, stir in the slurry, ghee, half-and-half, and lemon juice and let bubble for 30–60 seconds, then hit Keep Warm/Cancel again to turn off the pot. Stir in the Parmesan, parsley, and capers (if using).

7 Once the bubbles die down, spoon the sauce over the tilapia and serve topped with more capers, if desired.

JEFF'S TIPS Hate capers? I'll forgive you. Just leave 'em out and shave off about 65mg sodium per serving.

Because this is a keto recipe, you can use heavy cream instead of the nondairy milk.

FISH TACOS

Serves 6

PER SERVING
with/without sauce
Calories: **271/207**
Fat: **14.2g/9.6g**
Carbs: **5.4g/0.2g**
Sodium: **222mg/112mg**
Protein: **31.1g/30.4g**
Fiber: **0.6g/0.1g**
Sugars: **2.3g/0g**

 (if not making the sauce)

These fish tacos elevate Taco Tuesday to the next level. Plus, even with the cool, flavorful, and refreshing sauce drizzled on top of them, they're *still* on the lighter side! In fact, they're so delicious, you don't even need a tortilla to wrap the fish in—you can wrap it in some Bibb lettuce or serve over my Quintessential Quinoa (page 116)!

Prep Time	Pressure Building Time	Pressure Cook Time	Total Time
5 MIN	**5–10** MIN	**5** MIN	**15** MIN

THE FISH

2 pounds (1-inch-thick) skinless tilapia fillets

3 tablespoons extra-virgin olive oil

1/2 teaspoon ground cumin

1/2 teaspoon chili powder

1/2 teaspoon seasoned salt

THE SAUCE

1/2 cup low-fat sour cream or plain 2% Greek yogurt (store-bought or homemade, page 36)

Juice of 1 lime

1 teaspoon sriracha (optional)

1 teaspoon ground cumin

1 teaspoon garlic powder

1 teaspoon paprika

1 teaspoon dried cilantro (optional)

THE TACOS (OPTIONAL)

Corn or whole-wheat tortillas

Toppings, such as diced mango, hot sauce, shredded cabbage, diced red onion, fresh cilantro, sliced avocado, corn kernels, diced tomatoes, sliced black olives, and/or crumbled cotija or shredded low-fat cheese

1 Place the trivet in the Instant Pot and pour in 1 cup of water. Place a parchment round on the trivet and lay the tilapia on the parchment (it's okay if the fillets rest on each other).

2 Mix the oil, cumin, chili powder, and seasoned salt in a bowl and lightly brush the mixture onto each tilapia fillet. Secure the lid, move the valve to the sealing position, and hit Manual or Pressure Cook on High Pressure for 5 minutes. Quick release when done.

3 Meanwhile, combine all the sauce ingredients in a bowl and set aside.

4 Carefully remove the trivet, place the fish on a cutting board, and let cool for a few moments before cutting into bite-size pieces.

5 Assemble your tacos as you see fit and drizzle with the sauce to give them a cool, delicious finish!

JEFF'S TIP You can use any fish you'd like for this. The pressure cooking time remains the same so long as the fillets are 1 inch thick.

SAFFRON SEAFOOD RISOTTO

Serves 6

PER SERVING
Calories: **306**
Fat: **13.4g**
Carbs: **19.6g**
Sodium: **420mg**
Protein: **18.9g**
Fiber: **0.2g**
Sugars: **1.3g**

Saffron, while one of the pricier spices on the market, is worth every penny as a small amount goes a very long way in many dishes. It sets the stage tremendously for this spectacular seafood-studded risotto.

Prep Time	Sauté Time	Pressure Building Time	Pressure Cook Time	Final Cook Time	Total Time
10 MIN	10 MIN	10–15 MIN	6 MIN	5 MIN	45 MIN

- **2 tablespoons extra-virgin olive oil**
- **2 tablespoons ghee (store-bought or homemade, page 39)**
- **1 teaspoon saffron**
- **2 large shallots, diced**
- **3 cloves garlic, minced or pressed**
- **2 cups Arborio rice (you must use Arborio to make a proper risotto)**

- **1 cup dry white wine (like a chardonnay) or additional broth**
- **4 cups Garlic Broth (page 44) or low-sodium vegetable broth**
- **½ pound raw large or jumbo shrimp, peeled and deveined**
- **½ pound fresh scallops (any size)**
- **½ pound calamari rings**

- **1 teaspoon dried oregano**
- **1 teaspoon Italian seasoning**
- **1 teaspoon seasoned salt**
- **1 teaspoon black pepper**
- **½ cup grated Parmesan cheese (optional)**
- **Fresh chives, for garnish (optional)**

1 Add the oil and ghee to the Instant Pot, hit Sauté, and Adjust so it's on the More or High setting.

2 Once the oil's bubbling and the ghee's melted (about 3 minutes), add the saffron and shallots and sauté for 2 minutes. Add the garlic and sauté for 1 minute.

3 Add the rice and stir for 1 minute, then add the wine and let simmer for 2 minutes. Add the broth and give it all a final stir.

JEFF'S TIP Should you like a bit more seafood flavor in the broth, go for lobster or fish broth (such as 4 teaspoons Lobster or Fish Better Than Bouillon plus 4 cups water). Either will increase the sodium by about 360mg.

4 Hit Keep Warm/Cancel, secure the lid, move the valve to the sealing position, and hit Manual or Pressure Cook on High Pressure for 6 minutes. Quick release when done.

5 Stir in the shrimp, scallops, calamari, oregano, Italian seasoning, seasoned salt, and pepper. Cook stirring, for 5 minutes, or until the shrimp are opaque and curled. Stir in the Parmesan (if using).

6 Serve topped with chives, if desired.

MUSSELS IN THAI COCONUT CURRY

Serves 8

PER SERVING
Calories: **284**
Fat: **12.5g**
Carbs: **13.3g**
Sodium: **703mg**
Protein: **27.5g**
Fiber: **0.7g**
Sugars: **0.2g**

Mussels are one of the things the Instant Pot does quickest and best. This Thai curry sauce is everything, I tell you. *Everything.*

Prep Time	Sauté Time	Pressure Building Time	Pressure Cook Time	Total Time
10 MIN	5 MIN	10–15 MIN	3 MIN	30 MIN

¼ cup ghee (store-bought or homemade, page 39)

2 large shallots, diced

2 stalks lemongrass (tender inner stalks only), sliced into short ¼-inch-thick strips

3 cloves garlic, minced or pressed

1 (13.5-ounce) can unsweetened light coconut milk (NOTE: Shake the can to make sure the coconut milk is thin like water, not thick and lumpy.)

2 tablespoons coconut aminos, low-sodium soy sauce, or tamari

2 teaspoons curry powder

1½ teaspoons dried parsley

1 teaspoon seasoned salt

1 teaspoon ground ginger

½ teaspoon ground turmeric

3–5 pounds fresh mussels, rinsed and debearded (make sure to toss out any that have already opened before cooking)

Juice of 1 lime

1 bunch fresh tarragon, stems removed

1 Add the ghee to the Instant Pot, hit Sauté, and Adjust so it's on the More or High setting. Once it's melted and bubbling (about 3 minutes), add the shallots and lemongrass and sauté for 2 minutes. Add the garlic and sauté for 1 minute.

2 Add the coconut milk, coconut aminos, curry powder, parsley, seasoned salt, ginger, and turmeric and stir well.

3 Add the mussels (in this case, you can fill the pot to the brim so long as there's room for the lid), squeeze the lime juice over them, and top with the tarragon leaves (reserve a few for garnish). Secure the lid, move the valve to the sealing position, and hit Manual or Pressure Cook on High Pressure for 3 minutes. Quick release when done. Toss any mussels that haven't opened after cooking.

4 Transfer the mussels and sauce to a large serving dish and serve immediately, garnished with the reserved tarragon.

JEFF'S TIP If you want a slightly sugary-sweet flavor, sub in fish sauce for the coconut aminos, but use only 1 tablespoon.

8

VEGETABLES & SIDES

How could this be a lighter cookbook without
a bunch of delicious veggie dishes? In this chapter we'll
explore some healthy options to serve as both
mains and sides and that taste so absolutely glorious you'll
forget they're also good for you.

= AIR FRYER LID = DAIRY-FREE

 = KETO = GLUTEN-FREE

P = PALEO V = VEGETARIAN

+ = COMPLIANT WITH MODIFICATIONS  VN = VEGAN

TOFU TIKKA MASALA

Serves 6

PER SERVING
Calories: **230**
Fat: **15.2g**
Carbs: **15.4g**
Sodium: **165mg**
Protein: **10.4g**
Fiber: **3.4g**
Sugars: **8.5g**

 K + *(if using monk fruit sweetener)*
GF
V

If you're a lover of Indian cuisine, you'll know that a creamy, tomato-based tikka masala usually tops the list of the most popular items ordered. It took a lot to tear me away from chicken as my protein, but I quickly discovered that tofu makes for a wonderful replacement. Not to mention, the sauce is as mouthwatering as they come. I like to serve this over my Cilantro-Lime Basmati Rice (page 130).

Prep Time	Sauté Time	Pressure Building Time	Pressure Cook Time	Total Time
5 MIN	11 MIN	10–15 MIN	2 MIN	35 MIN

- **¼ cup refined coconut oil or extra-virgin olive oil**
- **2 (14–16-ounce) packages extra-firm tofu** (NOTE: It must be extra-firm to hold its form), **drained and cut into ½-inch cubes, divided**
- **1 medium yellow onion, diced**
- **3 cloves garlic, minced or pressed**
- **1 (13.5-ounce) can unsweetened light coconut milk** (NOTE: Shake the can to make sure the coconut milk is thin like water, not thick and lumpy.)

- **1 cup no-salt-added canned crushed tomatoes**
- **2 tablespoons garam masala, divided**
- **3 teaspoons seasoned salt, divided**
- **2 teaspoons ground cumin, divided**
- **½ teaspoon ground turmeric, divided**
- **½ cup loosely packed chopped fresh cilantro, plus more for topping (optional)**

- **1 bay leaf**
- **½ cup plain 2% Greek yogurt (store-bought or homemade, page 36)**
- **1 (8-ounce) can no-salt-added tomato sauce (not the same as pasta sauce)**
- **1 tablespoon monk fruit sweetener or pure maple syrup**
- **½ teaspoon cayenne pepper (optional)**

1 Add the oil to the Instant Pot, hit Sauté, and Adjust so it's on the More or High setting. After 3 minutes of heating, add half of the tofu and gently sauté for 5–10 minutes, until the tofu is very lightly browned. Add the onion and garlic and sauté for 3 minutes.

2 Add the coconut milk, crushed tomatoes, 1 tablespoon of the garam masala, 1 teaspoon of the seasoned salt, 1 teaspoon of the cumin, ¼ teaspoon of the turmeric, and cilantro (if using). Mix until well combined, deglazing the bottom of the pot to make sure it's free and clear of any browned bits. Top with the bay leaf.

3 Secure the lid, move the valve to the sealing position, hit Keep Warm/Cancel, and then hit Manual or Pressure Cook on High Pressure for 2 minutes. Quick release when done and remove the bay leaf.

4 Add the remaining tofu, yogurt, tomato sauce, sweetener or maple syrup, remaining 1 tablespoon of garam masala, remaining 2 teaspoons of seasoned salt, remaining 1 teaspoon of cumin, remaining ¼ teaspoon of turmeric, and cayenne (if using). Stir until well combined, then let rest for 5 minutes to thicken slightly.

5 Serve topped with additional cilantro, if desired.

JEFF'S TIPS If you have the time (perhaps while prepping other ingredients), I suggest you press your tofu so it will stay firm and absorb even more of the delicious sauce. Before dicing the tofu, line a rimmed baking sheet with a few paper towels and place the tofu bricks on top. Then place a heavy wooden cutting board (or anything else with substantial weight, like a skillet plus a few cans of tomatoes) on top of it. Leave for 10–15 minutes, until most of the moisture is squeezed out of the tofu.

The reason we add some tofu before pressure cooking and some after is for texture—you get the best of both worlds with both softer and slightly chewier tofu!

ACORN SQUASH MASH

Serves 6

PER SERVING
Calories: **134**
Fat: **7.7g**
Carbs: **16.2g**
Sodium: **210mg**
Protein: **2.7g**
Fiber: **2.4g**
Sugars: **0.1g**

 + *(if using nondairy milk)*

GF

V

Acorn squash is the sweeter friend of butternut squash, and it makes for the most amazing, sweet mash to go with any dish—or simply on its own. It is especially wonderful in the harvest months for its color and fall-inspired flavor.

Prep Time	Pressure Building Time	Pressure Cook Time	Total Time
5 MIN	5-10 MIN	10 MIN	25 MIN

1 cup Garlic Broth (page 44) or low-sodium vegetable broth

2 acorn squash, halved and seeded (choose carefully at the market to ensure they'll fit in your Instant Pot)

3 tablespoons ghee (store-bought or homemade, page 39)

½ cup unsweetened nondairy milk, fat-free half-and-half, or 2% dairy milk (you can use more if you want it creamier)

3 cloves garlic, minced or pressed, or Roasted Garlic (page 42)

¼ cup grated Parmesan cheese, plus more for serving (optional)

2 teaspoons seasoned salt

1 teaspoon black pepper, plus more for serving

1 teaspoon curry powder (optional)

1 Place the trivet in the Instant Pot, pour in the broth, and rest the squash halves on top, skin-side down. Secure the lid, move the valve to the sealing position, and hit Manual or Pressure Cook on High Pressure for 10 minutes. Quick release when done.

2 Carefully remove the cooked squash with tongs and set aside to cool.

3 Once the squash is cooled (about 5 minutes), scoop all the flesh into a large mixing bowl and discard the skins. Pour in about a third of the broth from the pot and use a potato masher to mash to the desired consistency.

4 Add the ghee, milk, garlic, Parmesan (if using), seasoned salt, pepper, and curry powder (if using) and stir into the mash until combined.

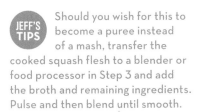

5 Serve topped with additional Parmesan, if desired, and pepper.

JEFF'S TIPS Should you wish for this to become a puree instead of a mash, transfer the cooked squash flesh to a blender or food processor in Step 3 and add the broth and remaining ingredients. Pulse and then blend until smooth.

In addition to a wonderful side, this also makes a great baby food (just use your judgment on the additional ingredients)!

SLOPPY JOSEPHINES

Eating healthier doesn't mean giving up the foods you love—it can just mean learning to make them with healthier ingredients. Speaking of which, did you know that Sloppy Joe has an herbivore sister named Sloppy Josephine? She replaces the meat with melt-in-your-mouth lentils. But don't leave the napkins behind. This dish gives you all the flavor and delightful mess of the original!

Serves 8

PER SERVING
Calories: **317**
Fat: **6.3g**
Carbs: **50.7g**
Sodium: **533mg**
Protein: **15.7g**
Fiber: **16.4g**
Sugars: **16.2g**

 DF
 GF
VN + *(if using fish-free steak sauce)*

Prep Time	Sauté Time	Pressure Building Time	Pressure Cook Time	Natural Release Time	Total Time
10 MIN	10 MIN	10–15 MIN	15 MIN	10 MIN	1 HR

- 3 tablespoons extra-virgin olive oil
- 1 small red onion, diced
- 1 green bell pepper, seeded and diced
- 1 medium carrot, peeled and diced
- 8 ounces baby bella or white mushrooms, finely chopped (optional)
- 3 cloves garlic, minced or pressed
- 1 teaspoon liquid smoke (optional)
- 2 tablespoons Worcestershire sauce or sugar-free steak sauce

- 2½ cups Garlic Broth (page 44) or low-sodium vegetable broth
- 1 (14.5-ounce) can no-salt-added diced tomatoes, with their juices
- 1 pound brown lentils, rinsed
- 1½ teaspoons seasoned salt
- 1½ teaspoons ground cumin
- 1 teaspoon chili powder (optional)
- 1 (8-ounce) can no-salt-added tomato sauce (not the same as pasta sauce)

- 2 tablespoons coconut aminos, low-sodium soy sauce, or tamari
- 2 tablespoons gluten-free hoisin sauce
- 1 tablespoon pure maple syrup or monk fruit sweetener
- 1 tablespoon Dijon mustard (optional)
- Whole-grain toast, whole-wheat buns, or whole-wheat wraps (optional)

1 Add the oil to the Instant Pot, hit Sauté, and Adjust so it's on the More or High setting. After 3 minutes of heating, add the onion, bell pepper, carrot, and mushrooms (if using) and sauté for 5 minutes. Add the garlic and liquid smoke (if using) and sauté for 1 minute.

2 Add the Worcestershire or steak sauce and scrape the bottom of the pot to loosen any browned bits.

3 Add the broth, tomatoes, lentils, seasoned salt, cumin, and chili powder (if using) and stir well.

4 Secure the lid, move the valve to the sealing position, hit Keep Warm/Cancel, and then hit Manual or Pressure Cook at High Pressure for 15 minutes. When done, allow a 10-minute natural release followed by a quick release.

5 Give everything a stir and then add the tomato sauce, coconut aminos, hoisin sauce, maple syrup, and mustard (if using). Stir until well combined and let rest for 5 minutes.

6 Serve on whole-grain toast, whole-wheat buns, or whole-wheat wraps, if desired.

JEFF'S TIP Feel free to top these off with some sliced tomato, shredded lettuce, and/or the shredded low-fat cheese of your choice.

CHANA SAAG
(SPINACH CHICKPEA CURRY)

Serves 6

PER SERVING
Calories: **208**
Fat: **8g**
Carbs: **28.3g**
Sodium: **183mg**
Protein: **8.8g**
Fiber: **8.5g**
Sugars: **5.8g**

DF + *(if using olive oil)*

GF

VN + *(if using olive oil)*

Peppered with chickpeas and an array of exotic-tasting yet accessible ingredients found in basically any market, this Instant Pot take on the creamy spinach-chickpea Indian dish is a veggie lover's dream and makes for a wonderfully rich-tasting, yet light and easy, weekday lunch or dinner when served over rice (page 114).

Prep/Soaking Time	Sauté Time	Pressure Building Time	Pressure Cook Time	Natural Release Time	Total Time
8 HRS	5 MIN	10–15 MIN	20 MIN	5 MIN	8 HRS 45 MIN

1 cup dried chickpeas

2 tablespoons ghee (store-bought or homemade, page 39) or extra-virgin olive oil

1 medium yellow onion, diced

1½ teaspoons cumin seeds (optional)

3 cloves garlic, minced or pressed

1 (13.5-ounce) can unsweetened light coconut milk (NOTE: Shake the can to make sure the coconut milk is thin like water, not thick and lumpy.)

Juice of ½ lime

2 tablespoons garam masala, divided

2 teaspoons seasoned salt, divided

2 teaspoons ground cumin, divided

½ teaspoon ground turmeric

½ teaspoon ground cinnamon

12 ounces baby spinach, chopped

3 tablespoons no-salt-added tomato paste

1 Put the chickpeas in a large pot or mixing bowl, add about 4 cups of warm water, and cover. Allow to soak at room temperature for 8 hours.

2 After soaking, you'll see the chickpeas will have nearly doubled in size! Drain and rinse the chickpeas in a strainer and set aside.

3 Add the ghee or olive oil to the Instant Pot, hit Sauté, and Adjust so it's on the More or High setting. Once heated (about 3 minutes), add the onion and cumin seeds (if using) and sauté, stirring occasionally, for 3 minutes, or until slightly softened. Add the garlic and sauté for 1 minute.

4 Add the chickpeas, coconut milk, lime juice, 1 tablespoon of the garam masala, 1 teaspoon of the seasoned salt, 1 teaspoon of the ground cumin, the turmeric, and cinnamon and stir. Top with the spinach.

5 Secure the lid, move the valve to the sealing position, hit Keep Warm/Cancel, and then hit Manual or Pressure Cook on High Pressure for 20 minutes. When done, allow a 5-minute natural release followed by a quick release.

6 Add the tomato paste, remaining 1 tablespoon of garam masala, remaining 1 teaspoon of seasoned salt, and remaining 1 teaspoon of ground cumin and stir until well combined. Let rest for 5 minutes before serving.

JEFF'S TIP Didn't remember to soak the chickpeas ahead of time? No sweat. Use 2 (15.5-ounce) cans low-sodium chickpeas, drained and rinsed. Shave the pressure cook time down to 10 minutes and allow a quick release.

MEXICAN STREET CORN (ELOTE)

Serves 6

PER SERVING

with /without sauce

Calories: **282/143**

Fat: **13.7g/2.2g**

Carbs: **34.6g/31g**

Sodium: **478mg/25mg**

Protein: **11.5g/5.4g**

Fiber: **3.8g/3.3g**

Sugars: **11.1g/10.4g**

This is one of those dishes that just tastes better the messier you get while eating it. Mexican street corn (also known as elote) is something that you'll find at food trucks and carnivals, and now right in your Instant Pot. And it's as addictive as it is simple to make. This version allows you to get the corn soft, then gives it a final roasting step in the oven or with the air fryer lid.

Prep Time	Pressure Building Time	Pressure Cook Time	Optional Roasting Time	Total Time
5 MIN	5-10 MIN	4 MIN	10-15 MIN	30 MIN

THE CORN

6 ears fresh corn, shucked

THE ELOTE SAUCE

⅓ cup low-fat mayonnaise

⅓ cup plain 2% Greek yogurt (store-bought or homemade, page 36) or low-fat sour cream

Juice of ½ lime, plus more for topping

¼ cup crumbled cotija cheese, plus more for topping

1 tablespoon dried cilantro, plus more for topping

1 teaspoon chili powder, plus more for topping if desired

1 Place the trivet in the Instant Pot, pour in 1 cup of water, and layer the corn in a crisscross fashion on top. Secure the lid, move the valve to the sealing position, and hit Manual or Pressure Cook on High Pressure for 4 minutes. Quick release when done and then hit Keep Warm/Cancel to turn the pot off.

2 While the corn is cooking, combine all the elote sauce ingredients in a bowl and set aside.

3 Using tongs, transfer the corn to a plate. **Optional Roasting Step:** Drain the liner pot, wipe it dry, and return it to the Instant Pot. Put the trivet and corn back in, two or three at a time. Add the air fryer lid, hit Broil (400°F) for 10–15 minutes, and hit Start to begin. Allow it to roast, rotating the corn midway through. If you want it roasted longer, air fry for longer. Alternatively, if you don't have an air fryer lid, place the pressure cooked corn on a foil-lined baking sheet and broil in the oven for 3–5 minutes, rotating it halfway through (keep an eye on it so it doesn't burn, as ovens vary).

4 If you want to get a little showy (and less messy while eating), insert a wooden skewer in the bottom of each ear, then slather the corn with the elote sauce. Top with additional cotija cheese, cilantro, squeezed lime, and chili powder if you so desire.

JEFF'S TIP If you can't find cotija cheese, you can use grated Parmesan or crumbled feta instead.

LEEKY LEMON BROCCOLI

Serves 4

PER SERVING
Calories: **146**
Fat: **7g**
Carbs: **20g**
Sodium: **48mg**
Protein: **4.1g**
Fiber: **4.4g**
Sugars: **5.4g**

K
P
DF + *(if using olive oil)*
GF
VN + *(if using olive oil)*

There's just something about broccoli covered in freshly squeezed lemon juice and then roasted until a bit charred that makes me want to eat it every day. Add some crispy leeks to the mix and suddenly I want to eat it at every meal. To make this a speedy side, the recipe utilizes only the pot's sauté function as well as the air fryer lid.

Prep Time	Sauté Time	Crisping Time	Total Time
5 MIN	**13** MIN	**10** MIN	**28** MIN

2 tablespoons ghee (store-bought or homemade, page 39) or extra-virgin olive oil

4 leeks (tender light green inner stalks only), cut into ¼-inch-thick slices

1 large head broccoli florets, cut into bite-size pieces

Juice of 1 lemon

1 Add the ghee or olive oil to the Instant Pot, hit Sauté, and Adjust so it's on the More or High setting.

2 Once it's melted and bubbling (about 3 minutes), add the leeks and sauté for 10 minutes. They will unravel while being stirred. (NOTE: Don't worry if some of the leeks look burnt—they taste even better with a bit of a char!)

3 Meanwhile, put the broccoli florets in a microwave-safe bowl, add about ¼ inch of water, cover with plastic wrap, and microwave for 3–4 minutes, until tender (if frozen, microwave for 9–10 minutes). Drain.

4 Add the broccoli to the pot and stir. Squeeze the lemon juice all over everything. Hit Keep Warm/Cancel to turn the pot off.

5 Add the air fryer lid, hit Broil (400°F) for 10 minutes, and hit Start to begin. Allow it to roast, stirring midway through. If you want it roasted longer, air fry for longer.

6 Transfer the veggies to a serving dish and enjoy.

JEFF'S TIP If you don't have the air fryer lid, turn the oven to broil, place the veggies on a foil-lined baking sheet, and broil for 5–10 minutes (keep an eye on them so they don't burn, as ovens vary).

CAULIFLOWER ALIGOT

Serves 6

PER SERVING
Calories: **275**
Fat: **20.5g**
Carbs: **10.5g**
Sodium: **281mg**
Protein: **14.3g**
Fiber: **3.6g**
Sugars: **4g**

Aligot is a French mashed potato dish so loaded with cheese, it stretches like taffy. However, since this is a *lighter* cookbook I feel less guilt about modifying such a beloved French recipe. To make a fair trade, I swap out the potatoes for cauliflower while still keeping a good amount of cheese, making it a keto-lover's dream. This is also the one recipe in this book that calls for heavy cream (because, again, keto). Just try to keep your portions in check with this one (wink wink). This goes really well with my Epic Balsamic Chicken (page 162).

Prep Time	Pressure Building Time	Pressure Cook Time	Sauté Time	Total Time
5 MIN	5–10 MIN	4 MIN	3 MIN	20 MIN

- **1 large head cauliflower, stalk and greens removed, florets cut into large chunks**
- **1 tablespoon ghee (store-bought or homemade, page 39)**

- **½ cup heavy cream (hey, it's keto, but see Jeff's Tips)**
- **2 teaspoons seasoned salt**
- **1 teaspoon black pepper**

- **1 teaspoon garlic powder**
- **2 cups shredded Gruyère or Swiss cheese**
- **1 cup shredded part-skim mozzarella cheese**

1 Place the trivet in the Instant Pot, pour in 1 cup of water, and place the cauliflower on top.

2 Secure the lid, move the valve to the sealing position, and hit Manual or Pressure Cook on High Pressure for 4 minutes. Quick release when done.

3 Transfer the cauliflower to a food processor or blender. Discard the water from the liner pot and return it to the Instant Pot (no need to wipe the inside).

4 Add the ghee, cream, seasoned salt, pepper, and garlic powder to the food processor or blender. Pulse and then blend into a smooth puree.

5 Return the mixture to the Instant Pot. Hit Keep Warm/Cancel, hit Sauté, and Adjust so it's on the Normal or Medium setting. After 3 minutes of heating, add the cheeses and stir until fully combined and the cheese stretches like taffy.

6 Transfer to a serving dish and serve immediately.

JEFF'S TIPS If you want this a bit lighter, sub half-and-half or fat-free half-and-half for the cream. Just know it technically no longer makes it keto-compliant due to the sugars in the half-and-half.

Aligot is best eaten immediately after it's made to ensure that the cheese is still stretchy and spectacular.

COLLARD GREENS

Serves 4

PER SERVING
Calories: **167**
Fat: **8.7g**
Carbs: **8.2g**
Sodium: **253mg**
Protein: **12.6g**
Fiber: **3.3g**
Sugars: **1.5g**

When the South came to pay my New York kitchen a visit (thanks to my partner, Richard, who is from Alabama), I was introduced to the simplicity of making collard greens in the Instant Pot. In typical Southern fashion, I've paired them here with a smoky ham hock, and I have to say: this dish is rip-snortin' good.

Prep Time	Pressure Building Time	Pressure Cook Time	Total Time
5 MIN	**5–10** MIN	**60** MIN	**1** HR 10 MIN

1 smoked ham hock

1 medium yellow onion, diced

6 cloves garlic, minced or pressed

4 cups low-sodium vegetable broth

1 pound collard greens, bottom stalks removed, veins intact and leaves cut into small pieces (kitchen shears work wonders for this)

½ teaspoon kosher salt

½ teaspoon seasoned salt

Hot sauce, for topping (optional)

1 Put the ham hock, onion, and garlic in the Instant Pot and pour in the broth.

2 Top with the collard greens. Press the greens down a bit, but don't worry if they are too close to the lid—they cook down significantly. *Do not stir* them up with the broth.

3 Secure the lid, move the valve to the sealing position, hit Keep Warm/Cancel, and then hit Manual or Pressure Cook on High Pressure for 60 minutes. Perform a quick release when done. (NOTE: They may smell a little pungent when quick releasing. That means you've done 'em right!)

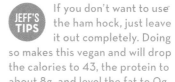
If you don't want to use the ham hock, just leave it out completely. Doing so makes this vegan and will drop the calories to 43, the protein to about 8g, and level the fat to 0g. The flavor won't be quite as special, however.

My Southern partner, Richard, informed me that the leftover broth in the pot is known as "pot liquor." Spoon it over some Cilantro-Lime Basmati Rice (page 130) for a delectable treat!

4 Use tongs to remove the ham hock and feel free to pick off the meat for garnish. Add the kosher salt and seasoned salt and stir. Let cool for 10 minutes, then serve with a few dashes of hot sauce and the reserved ham, if desired.

STUFFED ARTICHOKES

Serves 4

PER SERVING
Calories: **262**
Fat: **17.4g**
Carbs: **21.8g**
Sodium: **531mg**
Protein: **9.5g**
Fiber: **7.9g**
Sugars: **2.3g**

Artichokes stuffed with garlic, cheese, and seasonings? Yes, please! These aren't only fun to eat, but they make for a totally gorgeous presentation with minimal work. After tearing through the artichoke, don't forget to eat the heart at the bottom.

Prep Time	Pressure Building Time	Pressure Cook Time	Total Time
15 MIN	**5–10** MIN	**15–20** MIN	**35** MIN

4 small to medium artichokes

3/4 cup grated Parmesan cheese

1/4 cup whole-wheat or regular breadcrumbs (I find panko too coarse for this recipe)

1 tablespoon granulated garlic or garlic powder

2 teaspoons seasoned salt

2 teaspoons black pepper

1 teaspoon Italian seasoning

1 teaspoon dried oregano

1 1/2 cups water

3 cloves garlic, minced or pressed

1/4 cup extra-virgin olive oil

1 Let's give those artichokes a haircut! Chop off the stem with a knife, then snip off the thorny tip of each artichoke leaf with kitchen shears. When done, rinse them off and set aside to dry.

2 Mix together the Parmesan cheese, breadcrumbs, granulated garlic, seasoned salt, pepper, Italian seasoning, and oregano in a small bowl.

3 Place the trivet in the Instant Pot, then add the water and minced garlic.

CONTINUES

4 Holding one artichoke at a time over the pot, spread the leaves open and add one-fourth of the Parmesan-breadcrumb mixture, pressing it in between the leaves, then set the artichoke on the trivet. (Any mixture that falls off the artichokes will go into the water in the pot—which will become our dipping sauce.) Squeeze the artichokes together so they fit as well as possible; a 6-quart model should accommodate 4 artichokes.

5 Drizzle the oil all over the artichokes until it seeps into the petals.

6 Secure the lid, move the valve to the sealing position, and hit Manual or Pressure Cook on High Pressure for 15–20 minutes (15 for a slightly firmer bite or up to 20 if you want the artichokes very soft). Quick release when done. Use tongs to carefully transfer the artichokes to a plate.

8 Serve immediately. Each leaf should easily pull out. Dunk a leaf into the dipping sauce, skin the meat off with your teeth, then discard the leaf. Then eat the heart if you're willing to work to get it out (some say this is the hidden treasure of the artichoke!).

JEFF'S TIP If you wish to give the artichokes a crisp, here's what to do: After pressure cooking, feel free to sprinkle on a few additional shakes of Parmesan and breadcrumbs. Add the air fryer lid, hit Broil (400°F) for 5 minutes, and hit Start to begin. This will give them a lovely broiled look. You can also do this in the oven by placing the pressure cooked artichokes on a foil-lined baking sheet and broiling for 3–5 minutes (just keep an eye on them, as ovens vary).

7 The water will have darkened and become the dipping sauce for your artichokes. Pour it into a bowl.

ZUCCHINI CHIPS & TZATZIKI DIP

Serves 6

PER SERVING
with/without tzatziki dip
Calories: **185/77**
Fat: **12.5g/5g**
Carbs: **10.5g/5.5g**
Sodium:
287mg/116mg
Protein: **9.6g/3.6g**
Fiber: **2.2g/1.4g**
Sugars: **3.6g/1.3g**

In addition to giving some dishes a final crisp or broil, the air fryer lid can also be used on its own with no pressure cooking steps, transforming your Instant Pot into an air fryer! And when my partner, Richard, grew a zucchini the size of an arm in his garden, I knew I had to make a crispy zucchini chips recipe. This snack will prove that air-fried food can taste just as delicious as deep-fried.

Prep Time	Air Frying Time	Total Time
10 MIN	**30** MIN (IN 3 BATCHES AT 10 MINUTES PER BATCH)	**40** MIN

THE TZATZIKI DIP

- 1 cup plain 2% Greek yogurt (store-bought or homemade, page 36)
- ¼ seedless (English) cucumber, semi-peeled (striped) and diced
- 2 cloves garlic, minced or pressed
- ¼ cup loosely packed chopped fresh dill
- 1½ tablespoons extra-virgin olive oil
- 1 tablespoon red wine vinegar

- 1 tablespoon pesto sauce (optional and totally unconventional, but it gives the dip a wonderful extra "oomph." I love mine, page 208, but Costco's is great if you need some in a pinch.)
- ½ teaspoon Cavender's Greek Seasoning (optional)
- ½ teaspoon seasoned salt
- ½ teaspoon garlic powder

THE ZUCCHINI CHIPS

- ⅓ cup whole-wheat flour
- 1 teaspoon garlic powder
- 1 teaspoon paprika

- 1 teaspoon Italian seasoning
- 2 teaspoons seasoned salt
- ½ teaspoon black pepper
- 2 large eggs
- 2 teaspoons kosher salt
- ¾ cup panko breadcrumbs, or more as needed
- 2 tablespoons grated Parmesan cheese or nutritional yeast
- 1 large zucchini, cut into ¼-inch-thick disks (make sure they are all exactly this thick for even cooking)

CONTINUES

1 First, mix all the tzatziki dip ingredients in a bowl until combined. Cover and refrigerate until ready to serve.

2 To make the zucchini chips, grab 3 bowls. In bowl 1, whisk together the flour, garlic powder, paprika, Italian seasoning, seasoned salt, and pepper. In bowl 2, beat the eggs and kosher salt. And in bowl 3, whisk together the breadcrumbs and Parmesan.

3 One by one, coat each zucchini chip in the flour mixture (bowl 1), then dip in the egg (bowl 2), and finally coat in the breadcrumb mixture (bowl 3). Set aside.

4 Place the air fryer basket in the liner pot of the Instant Pot and spray with nonstick cooking spray. Spray the second rack too.

5 Working in batches as necessary, place the chips in a single layer in the basket. Lightly mist with olive oil spray. Once the bottom layer is filled, add the second rack and do the same.

6 Add the air fryer lid, hit Broil (400°F) for 10 minutes, and hit Start to begin. (NOTE: This is optional, but halfway through you can switch the top rack of chips with the bottom rack and then flip the chips for even cooking. Be sure to lightly mist the other sides again before resuming air frying.)

7 After 10 minutes of air frying, make sure the chips are crisped to the desired doneness. If not, go for longer.

8 Serve with the tzatziki for dipping.

JEFF'S TIP

If you don't feel like air frying in the Instant Pot in batches or don't have the air fryer lid, you can bake the chips in the oven. Preheat the oven to 425°F and line a rimmed baking sheet with aluminum foil, then mist it with nonstick cooking spray. Spread out the breaded zucchini chips in a single layer and bake for about 5 minutes, then flip and bake for another 5 minutes, or until nicely browned. Just keep an eye on them, as ovens vary.

EGGPLANT TOMATO DIP

Serves 6

PER SERVING
Calories: **102**
Fat: **3.2g**
Carbs: **18.9g**
Sodium: **350mg**
Protein: **3.8g**
Fiber: **7.7g**
Sugars: **10g**

This recipe is a favorite because it's as versatile as it is nutritious. Typically found at an Italian antipasto bar, caponata is a dip that is equally wonderful when scooped up with your favorite veggies or whole-grain chips, or spread on a toasted baguette or sandwich. I up the flavor by adding some sun-dried tomatoes in my version.

Prep Time	Pressure Building Time	Pressure Cook Time	Total Time
5 MIN	5–10 MIN	6 MIN	20 MIN

2 medium eggplants, peeled and sliced into ½-inch-thick disks

1 (10-ounce) jar sun-dried tomatoes, drained and diced, with 1 tablespoon oil reserved

1 tablespoon extra-virgin olive oil

Juice of ½ lemon

3 cloves garlic, minced or pressed

1 teaspoon dried oregano

1 teaspoon Italian seasoning

1 teaspoon seasoned salt

½ teaspoon black pepper

1 Pour 1 cup of water in the Instant Pot, lay in the trivet or steamer basket, and place the eggplant slices on top, piled up on top of each other.

2 Secure the lid, move the valve to the sealing position, and hit Manual or Pressure Cook on High Pressure for 6 minutes. Quick release when done.

5 Cover and chill in the fridge for up to 4 hours before serving.

JEFF'S TIP I also enjoy this caponata-like dip with capers or pitted and sliced kalamata olives mixed in. Start with 1 tablespoon and add more to taste, if desired.

3 Carefully remove the eggplant slices with tongs and transfer to a mixing bowl, draining any excess liquid. Mash with a potato masher until it's the desired consistency.

4 Add the sun-dried tomatoes with reserved oil, olive oil, lemon juice, garlic, oregano, Italian seasoning, seasoned salt, and pepper and mix until well-combined.

BLISTERED SHISHITO PEPPERS WITH YOGURT CURRY SAUCE

Serves 4
Per serving
with/without sauce
Calories: **103/38**
Fat: **3.9g/3.5g**
Carbs: **14.1g/7.6g**
Sodium: **76mg/0mg**
Protein: **4.2g/2.5g**
Fiber: **5.7g/5g**
Sugars: **9.9g/5g**

 + *(if only making the peppers)*
 + *(if only making the peppers)*
 GF
 + *(if only making the peppers)*

Few things give me as much joy as popping a pepper with a crispy, blistered skin into my mouth. One bite and a capsule of flavor bursts in your mouth. The secret is giving them a quick pressure cook to soften them before blistering. Not only do they make such a satisfying snack, but they're also good for you! As for the heat, they range from mild to medium-spicy.

Prep Time	Pressure Building Time	Pressure Cook Time	Crisping Time	Total Time
2 MIN	5–10 MIN	1 MINUTE	10–15 MIN	22 MIN

THE YOGURT CURRY SAUCE
¼ cup plain 2% Greek yogurt (store-bought or homemade, page 36)

Juice of ½ lemon

1½ teaspoons Dijon mustard

1 teaspoon raw honey

1 teaspoon curry powder

¼ teaspoon seasoned salt

¼ teaspoon dried dill

¼ teaspoon ground ginger

¼ teaspoon ground cumin

THE SHISHITO PEPPERS
1 pound whole shishito peppers

1 tablespoon extra-virgin olive oil

Sea salt, for topping (optional)

1 In a large bowl, combine all the yogurt curry sauce ingredients, cover, and pop in the fridge.

2 Pour 1 cup of water into the Instant Pot. Place the peppers in a steamer basket and lower into the pot. Secure the lid, move the valve to the sealing position, hit Keep Warm/Cancel, and then hit Manual or Pressure Cook on High Pressure for 1 minute. Quick release when done.

3 Remove the liner pot and transfer the peppers to a serving bowl. Drain the liner pot, pat it dry, and return it to the Instant Pot.

JEFF'S TIPS If you don't have the air fryer lid, simply transfer the peppers to a foil-lined rimmed baking sheet, drizzle with the olive oil, and broil in the oven for 3–5 minutes, until the peppers have blistered (keep an eye on them, as all ovens vary).

4 Place the air fryer basket in the Instant Pot and place the peppers in it on the second rack (it's fine if they are on top of one another). Lightly brush the oil all over the peppers. Add the air fryer lid, hit Broil (400°F) for 10–15 minutes, and hit Start to begin. Flip the peppers halfway through and continue to air fry until fully blistered (see Jeff's Tips).

5 When the peppers are blistered, return to the serving bowl, top with sea salt (if desired), and serve with the sauce for dipping.

These peppers taste great when eaten right away, while still hot. But they also work really well cold if you wish to blend them up into a sauce or add them to a salad.

If a yogurt curry sauce isn't your style, simply omit it and sprinkle the peppers with some sea salt instead.

9

DESSERT

As another book comes to a close, I present you with a sweet send-off. These desserts are all simple to make and are sure to satisfy all your lighter sweet tooth cravings.

 = AIR FRYER LID DF = DAIRY-FREE

K = KETO GF = GLUTEN-FREE

P = PALEO V = VEGETARIAN

+ = COMPLIANT WITH MODIFICATIONS VN = VEGAN

PEACHES & CREAM

Serves 6

PER SERVING
Calories: **140**
Fat: **9.1g**
Carbs: **15.3g**
Sodium: **13.3mg**
Protein: **2.1g**
Fiber: **2.3g**
Sugars: **18g**

K P DF GF VN

One of the most amazing things about the Instant Pot is its ability to blanch. That means we cook something at a high temperature and then shock it by immediately plunging it into an ice bath to stop the cooking process. When doing this with a peach, the skin peels right off. Combine that with some sweet cream, and life is a but a dream.

Prep Time	Pressure Building Time	Pressure Cook Time	Total Time
15 MIN	**10–15** MIN	**1** MINUTE	**30** MIN

6 ripe peaches

1 cup solidified canned unsweetened coconut cream
(NOTE: Be sure not to shake the can so the cream remains separated. You can get 1 cup solidified cream from about two 13–15-ounce unshaken cans, using only the hardened top portion; discard the liquid below it.)

2 teaspoons monk fruit sweetener

¼ teaspoon vanilla extract

1 Place the trivet or steamer basket in the Instant Pot, pour in 1 cup of water, and place the peaches on top.

2 Secure the lid, move the valve to the sealing position, hit Keep Warm/Cancel, and then hit Manual or Pressure Cook on High Pressure for 1 minute. Quick release when done.

3 Use tongs to transfer the peaches to an ice bath (a large bowl filled with cold water and ice cubes) and let rest while you make the cream.

4 Combine the *solidified* coconut cream, sweetener, and vanilla in a mixing bowl with a hand mixer (or in a stand mixer with the whisk attachment). Beat on low speed and gradually work your way up to medium-high speed until stiff peaks form, 2–3 minutes.

5 Remove the peaches from the ice bath and pat dry. You should be able to peel the skins right off! Slice the peaches into wedges and discard the pits.

6 Put the peach wedges in a bowl, top with the cream, and serve.

JEFF'S TIP If you want a more indulgent and coconut-flavored topping, use sweetened instead of unsweetened coconut cream. But then there's no need for the sweetener or vanilla extract as the cream will have a sweet, coconut flavor.

MUG CAKES IN MASON JARS

These are so fun and easy to make that, well, an Instant Pot could do it. This adorable, nutritious cake tastes similar to a delightful pancake and is perfect for breakfast, dessert, or a snack. It's fully customizable based on the mix-ins, comes together right in the mini mason jar it is cooked in, and the recipe is easily doubled or quadrupled.

Serves 1

PER SERVING
Calories: **255**
Fat: **11.7g**
Carbs: **29.5g**
Sodium: **366mg**
Protein: **8.3g**
Fiber: **1.2g**
Sugars: **26.7g**

K + *(if using monk fruit sweetener)*
P
DF
GF
V

Prep Time	Pressure Building Time	Pressure Cook Time	Total Time
5 MIN	10–15 MIN	15–25 MIN	30–45 MIN

THE CAKE BASE

- **1/3 cup almond flour**
- **1 large egg**
- **2 tablespoons pure maple syrup or monk fruit sweetener**
- **1/2 teaspoon vanilla, almond, or lemon extract**
- **1/2 teaspoon refined coconut oil or ghee (store-bought or homemade, page 39), melted (optional)**
- **1/4 teaspoon baking powder**
- **1/8 teaspoon salt**
- **1/8 teaspoon ground cinnamon**

MIX-INS OF YOUR CHOICE

- **Fruits such as blueberries, raspberries, blackberries, strawberries, pomegranate arils, pineapple chunks, sliced bananas, and/or natural coconut**
- **Raw nuts such as almonds, pecans, and/or macadamias**
- **Seeds such as flax, chia, and/or hemp hearts (if using, add an equal amount of vegetable oil, as they absorb moisture)**
- **Carob chips, vegan chocolate chips, cacao powder, or unsweetened coconut flakes**

1 Combine the almond flour, egg, maple syrup or sweetener, extract, coconut oil or ghee (if using), baking powder, salt, and cinnamon in an 8-ounce mason jar. Stir *very* well to make sure all the flour is incorporated and not stuck to the sides and bottom.

2 Add any mix-ins of your choosing and stir well so they're mixed with the batter. Whatever you add, just make sure the jar isn't more than three-quarters of the way filled.

3 Cover the mason jar with aluminum foil (do *not* use the lid that came with the jar while pressure cooking).

4 Place the trivet in the Instant Pot, pour in 2 cups of water, and carefully rest the foil-topped mason jar on it.

5 Secure the lid, move the valve to the sealing position, and hit Manual or Pressure Cook on High Pressure for 15–25 minutes: 15 minutes will give you a runnier, more pudding-like consistency, 20 minutes will give you a light and fluffy-cake consistency, and 25 minutes will give you a dense and firm cake consistency. Quick release when done.

6 Immediately remove the foil from the jar and let cool for 10 minutes. Either serve right away or put the mason jar lid on the jar, pop in the fridge, and serve chilled.

 **JEFF'S TIPS** My favorite mix-ins combo is some blueberries, raspberries, and bananas. Feel free to drizzle with a little more maple syrup when serving.

You can fit up to 4 jars in a 6-quart Instant Pot; the pressure cooking time remains the same.

BANANA BREAD

Serves 8

PER SERVING
Calories: **236**
Fat: **10.2g**
Carbs: **40.8g**
Sodium: **264mg**
Protein: **5.1g**
Fiber: **2.5g**
Sugars: **23.1g**

 DF + *(if using coconut oil)*

 GF

V

My beautiful sister Amanda went bananas when she tried this gluten-free and super low-carb banana bread. In this masterpiece, I substitute almond flour for all-purpose and the difference really enhances the experience. It makes the banana bread as moist as can be, with not a dry edge in any bite. No monkeying around.

Prep Time	Pressure Building Time	Pressure Cook Time	Natural Release Time	Cooling Time	Total Time
10 MIN	10–15 MIN	55 MIN	10 MIN	20 MIN	1 HR 45 MIN

3 very ripe bananas (with black spots all over)

3 large eggs

⅓ cup monk fruit sweetener

¼ cup pure maple syrup

2 tablespoons ghee (store-bought or homemade, page 39) or refined coconut oil, melted and cooled

1 tablespoon applesauce (store-bought or homemade, page 48)

1 teaspoon vanilla extract

1 teaspoon ground cinnamon

1 teaspoon baking powder

1 teaspoon baking soda

¼ teaspoon salt

3 cups almond flour

1 Use a potato masher or fork to mash the bananas in a large mixing bowl.

2 Add the eggs, sweetener, maple syrup, ghee or coconut oil, applesauce, vanilla, cinnamon, baking powder, baking soda, and salt. Use a stand or hand mixer and beat on low to medium speed until combined.

3 Add the flour and mix on low until combined.

4 Grease a 6-cup Bundt pan with nonstick cooking spray (don't forget to grease the center). Pour the batter in and lightly cover with aluminum foil. Poke a hole through the foil in the center of the pan so the steam can pass through it.

5 Place the trivet in the Instant Pot, pour in 2 cups of water, and carefully lower the Bundt pan onto the trivet. Secure the lid, move the valve to the sealing position, and hit Manual or Pressure Cook at High Pressure for 55 minutes. When done, allow a 10-minute natural release followed by a quick release. Let cool for 20 minutes (see Jeff's Tip).

6 Lightly loosen the edges of the Bundt with a silicone spatula. Cover the lip of the pan with a large plate and carefully flip it so the banana bread slides out onto it. Slice and serve!

JEFF'S TIP To me, banana bread is best enjoyed when fully cooled to room temperature. So I prefer to wait about 3 hours until cutting into it. Just wrap it in some foil or rest under a cake dome on the counter before unmolding it. But of course you can totally not listen to me and dig in as soon as it's ready!

LEMON OR LIME CURD

A tart and sweet treat awaits you. Lemon or lime curd is crazy easy to make, satisfies many purposes, and is a total crowd pleaser. In this version, we're making it way less fattening by using a sugar substitute. Serve on yogurt with some granola, in hot tea, over decadent desserts (see my first book for those), or right out of the jar on its own (look at this as an opportunity to flex those moderation muscles).

Makes about 4 cups

PER SERVING
(*1 tablespoon*)
Calories: **32**
Fat: **2.9g**
Carbs: **11.4g**
Sodium: **7mg**
Protein: **0.7g**
Fiber: **0.4g**
Sugars: **8.4g**

Prep Time	Pressure Building Time	Pressure Cook Time	Natural Release Time	Chilling Time	Total Time
10 MIN	10–15 MIN	10 MIN	15 MIN	4 HRS	4 HRS 45 MIN

1¼ cups monk fruit sweetener

6 tablespoons ghee (store-bought or homemade, page 39), melted

2 large eggs plus 2 large egg whites

1 cup fresh lemon or lime juice (from any combination of 8 lemons or 12 limes), plus 3 tablespoons grated zest

1 teaspoon vanilla or lemon extract

1 Combine the sweetener and ghee in a mixing bowl and beat on low speed with a hand or stand mixer to a sandy consistency, about 30 seconds. Add the eggs and egg whites and continue to beat on low until smooth, about 30 seconds. Add the juice, zest, and extract and beat on low for another 30 seconds.

2 Transfer the mixture to four 8-ounce mason jars, filling each no more than three-quarters of the way. Place the lid on each jar and screw it on, but not tightly.

3 Place the trivet in the Instant Pot, pour in 1½ cups of water, and rest the mason jars on the trivet. Secure the lid, move the valve to the sealing position, hit Keep Warm/Cancel, and then hit Manual or Pressure Cook on High Pressure for 10 minutes. When done, allow a 15-minute natural release followed by a quick release.

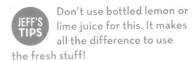
JEFF'S TIPS

Don't use bottled lemon or lime juice for this. It makes all the difference to use the fresh stuff!

If you want the curd to be less "pulpy," add less zest.

4 Remove the lids from the jars and mix with a fork until well combined. The curd should appear slightly frothy at this stage. Screw the lids back on each jar (this time tightly) and refrigerate for 4 hours for the curd to settle and thicken. Store in the fridge for up to 10 days.

BAKED APPLES

Serves 4

PER SERVING
Calories: **314**
Fat: **19.4g**
Carbs: **36.7g**
Sodium: **1mg**
Protein: **0.4g**
Fiber: **5.9g**
Sugars: **28.5g**

 GF

V

Baked apples are so glorious, beautiful, natural, and easy to make, of course I had to include them here. Coupled with some sweet spices, they taste exactly like that time of the year when leaves change color and start to fall.

Prep Time	Pressure Building Time	Pressure Cook Time	Natural Release Time	Total Time
10 MIN	5–10 MIN	5 MIN	5 MIN	30 MIN

⅓ cup old-fashioned oats (not instant)

6 tablespoons ghee (store-bought or homemade, page 39), melted

1 tablespoon pure maple syrup

1 tablespoon raw honey

1 teaspoon monk fruit sweetener

1 teaspoon vanilla extract

1 teaspoon ground cinnamon

⅛ teaspoon ground nutmeg

¼ cup raisins (optional)

¼ cup chopped raw nuts of your choice (optional)

4 medium apples (any kind will do, but I like Gala or McIntosh for these)

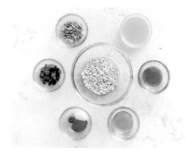

1 In a mixing bowl, combine the oats, ghee, maple syrup, honey, sweetener, vanilla, cinnamon, nutmeg, raisins (if using), and nuts (if using). Mix together until fully combined.

2 Core the apples, but don't go all the way through to the bottom.

3 Equally spoon the filling into the hole of each cored apple.

4 Place the trivet in the Instant Pot, pour in 1½ cups of water, and rest the stuffed apples on it. Secure the lid, move the valve to the sealing position, hit Keep Warm/Cancel, and then hit Manual or Pressure Cook on High Pressure for 5 minutes. When done, allow a 5-minute natural release followed by a quick release.

5 Carefully remove the apples (they will be very fragile) and serve on their own or however you wish!

JEFF'S TIP Of course you can serve this with a scoop of ice cream. But only as a reward if you've tried all the recipes in this book.

ACKNOWLEDGMENTS

Welp, that's another book in the books. (How did this happen when I said I was done after my first?!)

Apart from risking the biggest guilt trip ever should I not mention them first, I need to thank my mom and dad (again) for being my biggest cheerleaders. You've shown me a life that I am beyond fortunate to know and am beyond blessed to have you as mine.

To my dear Richard, who is my rock and always has a way of calming me down when I need it most (every other day isn't so bad, right?). Your wisdom, humor, and wit will always inspire me, and I am all the richer for having you by my side. There's a reason all my readers say, "We want more of Richard!" We all do. I'll always treasure our Friday nights of vinyl and whiskey.

To my wonderful sister, Amanda, who has given me some great advice on lighter eating since she has always known how to eat properly, unlike her prone-to-pudgy brother (that would be me). She's had two wonderful kids (hi, Levi and Stevie!) and was pregnant with her third at the time this book was written (hi to my future niece/nephew—I wanted to write your name since you're born as of this printing but your mommy and daddy didn't want to know your identity at the time I wrote this!). It's inspirational to see someone who has gone through the pregnancy game three times and still manages to whip back into shape.

To my dearly departed Grandma Lil for having been my source of cooking inspiration from the start. You always had a magical way with people through the gift of humor, and I like to think I inherited some of that (since I also inherited your waistline).

To my editor, Michael Szczerban, for approaching me to do this book four months before the first book even came out. Some may say you're a big gambler for that, but I'll now sit next to you at any blackjack table. I am very fortunate to have an editor who truly shares my vision and helps bring it to life so meticulously. (And extra thanks for giving me my blue cover.)

To my associate editor, Thea Diklich-Newell, for doing such a great job at molding the manuscript and being so on top of the crazy (and tedious) photo process.

To my production editor, Pat Jalbert-Levine, and my copyeditor, Karen Wise, for paying precise attention to my words and making my grammar look super professional and perfectly cookbook-speak. It especially means a lot that you've respected my voice and let it shine through as intended.

To Kim Sheu, Jules Horbachevsky, and Stephanie Reddaway for all their marketing and PR efforts at Voracious/Little Brown.

To all the producers at *Good Morning America*, *Rachael Ray*, and The Food Network, for giving me some very valuable airtime and trusting me to be a sound voice of electric pressure cooking while being my crazy, loud, Jewish New Yorker self on TV.

To my literary agent, Nicole Tourtelot, for putting up the good fight and for encouraging me to write this book, even though I swore it wouldn't happen for at least another year (I see what you did there).

To Laura Palese for, once again, designing the most stunning cookbook I've ever seen. Seriously, you've revolutionized the cookbook game—just look at the reviews for book 1! Sure, I may be biased, but you literally took my vision and executed it so brilliantly to fit my tutorial-style approach, it was like you were in my head or something. I know your job wasn't easy, but you sure make it seem that way.

To Rodney Pruitt and Stefanie Daichendt for making sure I have the latest and greatest products from Instant Brands, as well as sending me fabulous, durable plates from Corelle, many of which are featured in the hero shots of this book.

To Joni Mowery, Gayle Bell, Amy DeLong Main, Melody Greenlaw, Keshia Huggins, Stacie Fournier, Marie Barkley, Monya Lester, Mellanie Garrett, and all the admins who've been there from the start for running the most successful, best, and resourceful Instant Pot groups on Facebook.

To April Seroda (my sista from anotha mista), Penny Shack, Kelly Winograd, and Sarah Constantino for giving me many useful tips on the keto and paleo lifestyles as I was researching how I would properly work them into this book. Your varied knowledge through your personal journeys on these subjects has been an enormous help.

To Amy Birnbaum for being the most encouraging friend and always making me feel like a million bucks.

To Mary-Louise Parker, for saying I could and should write. I don't think either of us expected it to be in the form of cookbooks, but I'll take it!

To Lexi Zozulya for, once again, capturing every last photo with style and *je ne sais quoi*. You are an army within the body of one person and I've been very lucky to have you play such an integral role in making both books come to life. (P.S. Extra thanks for the pointers to help perfect my borscht recipe! P.P.S. Did we seriously go through this twice in less than a year?!)

To Carol J. Lee for jumping right into the game so effortlessly and making my food look a million times better on a plate than I ever could. You are a magician and a gem, and it was a master class in food styling to watch you work.

To all my friends who've shown me kindness and support along the way, it will never go underappreciated nor will it be taken for granted. That's exactly why you're my friends.

And most importantly, if you've made it this far, I thank you, my reader. Whether you've been there from the first day I posted a video on YouTube in 2017 or you've just found me today through a Google search, thank you for buying this book. Thank you for taking this journey with me. Thank you for your time. This book simply would not be here if not for your support—and for that, I'll be forever grateful.

What are you
COOKING
TODAY?

INDEX

C

cabbage
Borscht, 86–87
Carolina Pulled Chicken with Slaw, 150–51
Mediterranean Chicken Stew, 82–83
pressure cook time, 57
Sesame-Peanut Quinoa Salad, 128–29
Cacio e Pepe Spaghetti Squash, 104–5
Cakes, Mug, in Mason Jars, 254–55
Cancel button, 25
Carnitas, Crispy, 180–82
Carolina Pulled Chicken with Slaw, 150–51
carrots
Carrot Bacon Chips, 52–53
Carrot & Shallot "Fried" Rice, 118–19
pressure cook time, 57
cauliflower
Cauliflower Aligot, 236–37
Cauliflower Rice & Broccoli Casserole, 126–27
Cream of Cauliflower, 76–77
pressure cook time, 57
replacing potatoes with, 21
rice, about, 11, 22
Roasted Garlic & Spinach Soup, 84–85
Stuffed Peppers, 175–77
celery, pressure cook time, 57
Chana Saag (Spinach Chickpea Curry), 230–31
cheese
adding to Instant Pot, 31
Black & Blue Soup, 74–75
Cacio e Pepe Spaghetti Squash, 104–5

Cauliflower Aligot, 236–37
Cauliflower Rice & Broccoli Casserole, 126–27
Greek Farro Feta Salad, 122–23
lighter versions of, 16
Mexican Street Corn (Elote), 232–33
Stuffed Artichokes, 240–42
cheese grater, 30
Chicago-Style Italian Beef, 190–92
chicken
Bubbe's Jewish Chicken Pot, 165–67
Carolina Pulled Chicken with Slaw, 150–51
Chicken Cacciatore, 138–40
Chicken Congee, 120–21
Chicken Fra Diavolo, 168–69
Chicken with Chinese Black Bean Sauce, 154–55
Chimichurri Chicken, 158–59
Creamy Avocado Chicken, 152–53
Dijon Dill Chicken, 156–57
dredging, 32
Epic Balsamic Chicken, 162–64
Herbaceous Roasted Chicken, 141–44
Jeffrey's Favorite Chicken, 145–47
Lemon Orzo Chicken, 148–49
Lemon Pepper Wings, 160–61
Mediterranean Chicken Stew, 82–83
Pesto Chicken Farfalle, 94–95
pressure cook times, 55
Stuffed Peppers, 175–77
White Chicken Chili, 62–64
Chicken Sausage & Peppers Pasta, 102–3
chickpeas
Chana Saag (Spinach Chickpea Curry), 230–31

Greek Farro Feta Salad, 122–23
Mediterranean Chicken Stew, 82–83
pressure cook time, 56
chile peppers
Pork Pozole, 65–67
Spectacular Salsa, 46–47
White Chicken Chili, 62–64
chili
Cuban Picadillo Chili, 193–95
White Chicken Chili, 62–64
Chimichurri Chicken, 158–59
Chinese Black Bean Sauce, Chicken with, 154–55
Chowder, Manhattan Clam, 80–81
Cilantro-Lime Basmati Rice, 130–31
clams
Linguine with Red Clam Sauce, 92–93
Manhattan Clam Chowder, 80–81
pressure cook time, 56
coconut aminos, about, 18
coconut flour, 20–21
coconut oil, 17
coconut sugar, 20
Collard Greens, 238–39
Congee, Chicken, 120–21
cooking charts
beans and legumes, 56
meat, 55
pasta, 54
poultry, 55
rice and grains, 54
seafood, 56
vegetables, 57
corn
Mediterranean Chicken Stew, 82–83

ALEKSEY ZOZULYA

ABOUT THE AUTHOR

Jeffrey Eisner is the author of the international bestseller
The Step-by-Step Instant Pot Cookbook and the creator of *Pressure Luck Cooking*,
an acclaimed, easy-to-follow Instant Pot recipe video blog. Featured
on the Food Network, *Good Morning America*, and *Rachael Ray*, he creates his
famously flavorful recipes at home. He enjoys Broadway musicals,
travel, eating pretty much everything, and spending time with his partner,
Richard, and their loving, sassy Norwich Terrier, Banjo.

PressureLuckCooking.com

Youtube.com/pressureluck

Facebook.com/pressureluckcooking

Instagram: @pressureluckcooking